THE
CEO
TEST

THE
CEO
TEST

MASTER THE CHALLENGES
THAT MAKE OR BREAK
ALL LEADERS

ADAM BRYANT & KEVIN SHARER

HARVARD BUSINESS REVIEW PRESS
BOSTON, MA

Library of Congress Cataloging-in-Publication Data

Names: Bryant, Adam, author. | Sharer, Kevin, 1948- author.
Title: The CEO test : master the challenges that make or break all leaders
    Adam Bryant and Kevin Sharer.
Description: Boston, MA : Harvard Business Review Press, [2021] | Includes
    index.
Identifiers: LCCN 2020038371 (print) | LCCN 2020038372 (ebook) | ISBN
    9781633699519 (hardcover) | ISBN 9781633699526 (ebook)
    Subjects: LCSH: Chief executive officers. | Executive ability. |
    Leadership.
Classification: LCC HD38.2 .B787 2021 (print) | LCC HD38.2 (ebook) | DDC
    658.4/2—dc23
LC record available at https://lccn.loc.gov/2020038371
LC ebook record available at https://lccn.loc.gov/2020038372

ISBN: 978-1-63369-951-9
eISBN: 978-1-63369-952-6

The paper used in this publication meets the requirements of the American National Standard for Permanence of Paper for Publications and Documents in Libraries and Archives Z39.48-1992.

To Jeanetta and Carol

Contents

Contents

THE
CEO
TEST

Introduction

Despite all the effort over the past several decades to understand what it takes to be an effective leader, the challenges
of leadership remain enormously difficult and elusive for
people at every level and across all types of organizations, from businesses to nonprofits to the public sector.

It is true for first-time managers, who often struggle to make the
transition from being a sole contributor to achieving through others.
How demanding should you be? When do you let go, and when do
you step in to do the work? How do you provide direct feedback without being too critical? How do you strike the right balance of being
friendly without trying to be just one of the gang? What are the right
moments to show vulnerability? Or is it always better to put up a
front of never-let-them-see-you-sweat confidence?

More-senior positions bring a whole new set of challenges. You
are now leading leaders. There are layers of managers below you
who all have to be aligned around shared goals, requiring constant

communication. You have to build and manage new networks of relationships across the organization. The expectations to deliver at a consistently high level can be unforgiving. The sheer volume of meetings, emails, and cross-department project deadlines become a test of endurance, as the work starts earlier, ends later, and bleeds more often into the weekend.

For those who become chief executive officers, the demands grow exponentially. The loneliness. The weight of responsibility. The relentless second-guessing and criticism. The pressure to have a leadership team of all stars who can also work together as an all-star team. The array of 24/7 demands that require extraordinary stamina to always be on, confident, and inspiring. The gray areas and trade-offs of tough decisions that often leave no one happy. The bubble that keeps bad news from reaching them. The demands from investors and board directors to deliver steady growth across every measure of performance. The expectation to always have the right answer when it can be hard just to figure out the right question.

But those pressures are not unique to the role of chief executive. We believe that *all* leaders face their own version of a CEO's tests; it's just that the intensity and consequences of those challenges grow as you move higher into roles with more breadth and complexity. That is why we will be sharing the stories, insights, and lessons from dozens of chief executives in this book—not because their jobs are unique, but because the universal challenges of leadership are brought into their highest and sharpest relief in the CEO position, providing the richest lessons for everyone who aspires to be a better leader. Simply put, we believe that learning how to lead like a CEO will make you more effective in your role today and lift the trajectory of your career.

We think we make a pretty good team for this project.

Adam has conducted in-depth interviews with more than six hundred CEOs and other leaders, starting with the weekly *Corner Office* interview series that he created for the *New York Times* (Kevin was among the first CEOs Adam interviewed). That series was launched with a different approach to interviewing chief executives. Rather than asking them about their strategies and industry trends, Adam has focused instead on timeless questions about the most important leadership lessons that the CEOs had learned. He interviewed leaders from all walks of life and backgrounds beyond the world of business—nonprofits, academia, government agencies, the military, and the world of entertainment. He interviewed well-known CEOs like Satya Nadella of Microsoft and Bob Iger of Disney, and young CEOs running small startups. And he interviewed a large percentage of women and minorities, but never asked them any gender- or race-specific questions because he wanted to interview everyone the same way, as leaders first and only.

Then in 2017, Adam joined Merryck & Co., an executive mentoring and senior leadership development firm, whose work with hundreds of clients over the past decade provides another deep well of experience from which we have drawn insights.

Kevin was president and then CEO of Amgen, the world's largest biotechnology company, over two decades, leading the company's expansion, almost entirely through organic growth, from $1 billion to nearly $16 billion in annual revenues. After stepping down from Amgen in 2012, he taught strategy and management at Harvard Business School for seven years and cocreated with his then faculty colleague and the current CEO of G.E., Larry Culp, and Nitin Nohria, the Harvard

Business School dean, a course on the life and role of the CEO and how to lead senior executive teams. He has served on the boards of Chevron, Unocal, Northrop Grumman, 3M, and in his roles as an executive, director, and mentor, he has been involved with more than twenty successful CEO transitions. While you will be hearing from dozens of chief executives in this book, we also will draw on Kevin's stories and insights—from his experiences that include serving as an officer in the US Navy and his rise up the ranks as an executive at McKinsey, General Electric, and MCI—to bring certain themes to life in several of the chapters. In effect, Kevin will serve as a player-coach in this book, as both coauthor and one of the CEOs sharing their experiences.

Though our backgrounds are very different, we are both wired as pattern spotters, and as we started working on the book, we spent endless hours discussing and debating the lessons that emerged from our respective experiences. To help guide our thinking, we drew up a list of questions to clarify our goals for the project:

- What are the critical challenges that make or break even the most promising executives?

- What lessons can be learned from those leadership challenges at the highest levels that can help all leaders perform better in their jobs?

- If you are going to invest time and energy to focus on becoming stronger as a leader, which aspects of leadership will provide the greatest return on that effort, whether you're a CEO or a first-time manager?

- What insights would be illuminating to business school students, useful to aspiring leaders, and provide fresh perspectives to CEOs and their leadership teams?

- Could we develop a shared language of leadership within companies that would be relevant to the work of leaders at all levels?

- Could we ensure that these insights are just as useful for leaders in the worlds of nonprofits and the public sector as they are for business executives?

In all candor, it took us several runs to distill the long lists that filled our whiteboards, but we started making faster progress once we adopted a useful metaphor of Russian nesting dolls to help guide our discussions. Many ideas that come up in leadership discussions, such as the importance of being trustworthy and also respecting others, are in fact quite similar, and we kept pushing ourselves to clarify which ideas could nest inside other ideas. We also decided to focus more on the tactical skills of leadership to create a kind of playbook on how to lead effectively, rather than focusing on the intrinsic qualities of effective leaders, like curiosity and self-awareness. After hours of healthy debate, we ultimately settled on the architecture of themes and subthemes that would best answer the questions in the bullet points.

The CEO test is not like an SAT test; it is more in the spirit of being tested by a difficult mountain climb. The challenges we describe in the chapters that follow are foundational to effective leadership, and they build on each other. Nobody can hope to succeed without a clear strategy, an effective leadership team, and a well-defined culture. From there, we will move into some of the finer points of leading others, like driving change and managing crises, and then shift to the inner game of leadership. Throughout the book, we will be noting the many paradoxes that help explain why straightforward answers can be so elusive for understanding leadership. Not only will the insights throughout this book make you a better leader, they will provide a simple, effective, and valuable lens for analyzing and assessing other leaders, teams, and companies.

To be clear, passing the CEO test does not mean scoring a perfect ten out of ten on each of the challenges that we describe. That would be unrealistic, as we all have our strengths and weaknesses. But we do believe that to succeed in a leadership role, you have to achieve a certain threshold level of proficiency in each of the skills in this book. Ignoring any one of them, or undervaluing their importance, can quickly cut short a leader's time in their chair. We know that there is so much leadership advice in the world that it can quickly lead to the "paralysis by analysis" of trying to remember the hundred different things you're supposed to do at any given moment. We are trying to help solve that problem by winnowing all that advice to this handful of critical themes, so that you will see the greatest impact on improving your leadership skills by working on these areas.

Because the focus of our book is on lessons from chief executives that are relevant for all leaders, there are many aspects of the CEO role that we are not going to address. If we were writing a book just for chief executives, we would include other key tests for them, including allocation of resources (expenses, capital, and people); mergers and acquisitions; managing the board of directors, investors, regulators, and customers; processes for high-stakes decisions; and building a product or service pipeline to ensure future financial and competitive success. Strategy requires making choices about what to do and what not to do, and we are choosing not to write about those topics in order to make this book as useful as possible to leaders at all levels.

Leadership is a big tent, with lots of room for different voices and approaches. So it's worth spending a bit more time to share our point of view about this sometimes bewildering topic, as it will inform everything in the pages that follow.

First, we are not fans of cookie-cutter, one-size-fits-all approaches to leadership. How you lead is going to depend broadly on three things:

- Your experience, capabilities, and personality

- The individual and collective capabilities and personalities of the people you're leading

- The context in which you're leading (small or big team? startup or legacy company? turnaround or hypergrowth?)

Right out of the gate, those three variables create an infinite number of permutations that make leading feel like an ever shifting, multilevel chessboard. And because leadership is so contextual, we are not going to traffic in shortcuts or fill-in-the-blank templates. Becoming an effective leader takes introspection and work, and the simplest questions of leadership—What is your strategy? What does success look like for your leadership team?—are often the most difficult to answer. What we can promise is that we will help speed up your learning curve and provide insights, stories, and tools for what matters most to lead effectively. The best leadership advice, after all, helps slow the game, so that you can better anticipate, understand, and label the nuanced dynamics of different situations in the moment and then guide them to better outcomes. We believe that our approach of sharing the stories, lessons, insights, and tips from veteran CEOs is the most effective way to impart that wisdom.

This book is meant to be interactive. At each turn, you'll have to decide how these insights apply to your situation and who you are as a leader. In that sense, this book, much like the leadership field itself, is a kind of Rorschach test. A new insight for you may be old hat to another reader. You might dismiss one example as not being applicable to your industry, while others will feel directly relevant. You may come across an insight that you've heard before but that you really needed to hear again at this particular moment. Our goal is to start conversations, not end them, and to provide guidance and frameworks to help refine your thinking and strategies on the aspects of leadership that matter most.

Our approach is more journalistic and practical than theoretical or ideological. One of the confounding features of the field of leadership is that anyone can say almost anything about leadership and they likely will be right at some level. In fact, very little that is written about leadership is wrong. But here's the rub: just because something isn't wrong doesn't mean it's an insight. The field is rife with platitudes and truisms, and people often talk about leadership in terms of what they *believe* is important. Those are discussions of ideology and do not readily lend themselves to debate, because it's like talking about what's important for leading a successful life rather than what's required for effective leadership. Yes, those lines can be blurry (authenticity is important in all aspects of life, including leadership), but we are going to make sharp distinctions between the two in this book and focus almost entirely on the skills and practices of effective leaders. We will not be engaging in philosophical discussions around the question of "What is leadership?" nor are we trying to add a new adjective in front of the word to coin a pithy phrase. Instead we'll focus on *how* to lead effectively. This is about mining the breadth and depth of experience of hundreds of accomplished leaders and bringing their insights and stories to life, often in their own words.

Though there are good leadership books that deal in scholarly frameworks, this is not a work of academic research, using quantitative data to support our findings. Our "data" is qualitative in nature, including the more than 6 million words of transcripts from Adam's interviews and the depth and breadth of Kevin's experience over a long career in leadership roles and as a mentor to CEOs and other senior executives. But from that qualitative data, clear patterns and themes emerged that we believe offer valuable insights on leadership. You will be the judge of whether we pass the test we have set for ourselves: to write a book that will help you be a more effective leader.

Leadership is getting harder, as the speed of disruption across all industries accelerates. We have a deep respect for the power of effective leaders to build organizations and bring out the best in the people who work for them, and we have seen too many examples of bad leaders tearing down organizations and inflicting emotional harm on employees. Our goal is to better prepare you to succeed, whether you're a CEO or just starting out in your career, by helping you master the most important tests of effective leadership. Let's get to work.

Test #1
Can You Develop a Simple Plan for Your Strategy?

Simplifying complexity is a leader's superpower.

What's the big idea, and so what?" As CEO of Amgen, Kevin, one of the authors, would often start meetings—typically one-on-ones with his senior leaders—with those bracing questions. He wasn't being snarky or rude, and he would often ask it with a smile. With others whom he didn't know so well, like a consultant coming into his office to pitch an idea, he would be more explicit about what he wanted, asking them for their big idea and then adding, "What do we do about it, and what will success look like?" In each case, he was laying down a challenge: Can you get to the point quickly by crystallizing the essence of your idea and why it's important? He had used other tactics over the years for the same effect, including invoking a metaphor to signal his expectations to his team: "It's your job to have a hypothesis of what the picture is," he would tell them. "Don't come into my office and dump jigsaw puzzles at my feet to start inventorying the pieces together. I want you to tell me what your hunch is about the picture. Truth is a mosaic, facts are the tiles, and we never have all the tiles." He would ask anybody who wanted to show him a forty-slide deck to set it aside and summarize what they were about to say. He was relentless about pushing responsibility back on others to connect the dots and to explain their ideas in simple, but not simplistic, terms—like the time his CFO walked into his office and suggested moving all their manufacturing to Puerto Rico. He explained, capturing his big idea and the "so what" in just a few sentences, that the tax incentives alone would have as much impact on the financials as a new blockbuster drug, and the move would eliminate the risk to its two California plants, which sat on top of the San Andreas Fault. After years of planning and hundreds of millions of dollars of investment, Amgen's major manufacturing operations are now based there.

Kevin developed this habit of relentlessly pushing for simplicity in his mid-twenties when he was the engineer officer of a fast-attack nuclear submarine. He had to be able to disassemble and reassemble the sub in his head, knowing every part and how they worked together, and how various catastrophic scenarios could unfold and how to fix them. That's when he started the practice of drawing what he jokingly called an "idiot diagram" for himself to explain how things work. His goal was to create the simplest, high-level framework for describing something that's breathtakingly complicated, from which he could progressively go deeper in terms of detail and be able to keep that 3D model in his head. Later in his career, when he joined Amgen, he had to quickly learn the science of biotechnology, something he had never studied. But Kevin was well versed in mechanical and electrical automatic control systems that were based on networks and multiple feedback loops, and he realized that the human body, at least systemically, worked a lot like a nuclear submarine. That insight created a framework for conversations with Amgen scientists about how different drugs would affect the body. He would never know as much as the scientists, of course, but he kept the discussion at an altitude that enabled him to understand both the science and the implications of potential new drugs for Amgen. "Reaching all the way back to my submarine days, I knew about automatic control systems," Kevin says. "So I could use that as a metaphor to understand biology. Then I could figure out the best five questions to ask."

Kevin's "big idea" provocation is a crucial test, arguably the most important one, that makes or breaks all leaders. It goes to the heart of the core skill of simplifying complexity, which is an essential tool for navigating and wringing insights from the onslaught of information and infinite choices that leaders face. It is the ability to quickly understand the conceptual essence of any issue—a high "get-it" factor—and to grasp its importance and implications. This ability to simplify complexity is a necessary time-management tool, a kind of Swiss Army knife of leadership that will make you more effective and more efficient by quickly bringing clarity to complex subjects that are fraught with ambiguity and risk, and it will help you bring people along with crystal-clear communications about various challenges and the strategies for tackling them. The skill of simplifying complexity is not widely shared, and leaders need to make a conscious effort to practice it themselves and demand it from others. This book is itself an exercise in simplifying complexity, as it is our attempt to distill the difficult art of leadership into a manageable set of insights and a concise guide for putting them into action.

A critical test of this skill for leaders is whether they can use it to articulate a clear, galvanizing plan for what the company is trying to achieve. Can they stand up in front of their employees and, in a simple and memorable way, explain where the company is headed and why, along with a plan, timetable, and ways to measure progress along the route? This is the cornerstone of any organization. Without clarity around a shared set of goals, and why they are important, leaders will struggle to align their team, leaving everyone to define for themselves what success looks like and how their work is contributing to the business. People may be working hard, but much of their energy will be wasted because the organization is out of sync, which in turn will encourage destructive silo behavior. So, this is the first CEO test that all leaders face: Can they create a clear and simple plan to get everyone moving in the same direction? "The leader's job is to simplify complexity, and be right," Kevin says. "It can't be simple and wrong. It has to be simple and right."

This theme was echoed often in one of the author's (Adam's) interviews with more than six hundred leaders, many of whom shared their observation that senior executives often have difficulties describing a clear vision. The same struggle shows up often in Merryck & Co.'s mentoring work with C-suite executives. Across hundreds of engagements, one of the thorniest conversations starts with the simple question, "What is your strategy?" It's not that the leaders don't have a plan; it's just much clearer to them than it is to everyone else.

Experienced board directors said they find that the skill is rare, as well. "The CEO might be passionate about some idea or vision, but they're actually not very clear on the destination," said Chris Brody, a former partner of the private equity firm Warburg Pincus, who has decades of experience investing in companies and serving on the boards of companies of all sizes, including Intuit. "If they can't describe it to anybody else, they are going to dissipate a lot of valuable resources getting there. I often see too much passion for an amorphous outcome, which confuses people."

"It's amazing how many times companies go down a rabbit hole where they really don't have a relevant point of difference or a real competitive advantage."
—Don Knauss, former CEO, The Clorox Company

Don Knauss, the former CEO of Clorox and a veteran board director, said he looks for clarity—in effect, the result of effectively simplifying complexity—from leaders to describe their company's "economic True North." As he explained it, "When you peel the onion back on whatever the company's articulating in terms of how they're going to win in the marketplace, it's about the 'right to win.' You have to have a relevant point of difference for the consumer. It's amazing how many times companies go down a rabbit hole where they really don't have a relevant point of difference or a real competitive advantage, either in their cost structure or in their capabilities, to win in the marketplace. And if you don't see that fundamental advantage, you can get a sense very quickly whether what they're advocating is smoke and mirrors or really has a chance of winning."

Why do so many executives struggle with this challenge? There are many reasons, but the biggest one starts with the fact that the word "strategy" can mean different things to different people. In our experience, when you ask somebody about their strategy, you are likely to hear answers that either are too lofty, like a mission and vision statement, or are a general description of what the company does, rather than a statement of what it is trying to achieve. Or their strategy goes to the other extreme, diving down into the weeds of a long list of short-term priorities and initiatives. What often is missing is the middle layer between too vague and too granular, something that we call, for lack of a better term, a simple plan.

In broad terms, the role of the simple plan is to help address two questions that every employee deserves an answer to: What should I be working on? Why is it important? The answer must meet a crucial standard: "It has to be crystal clear," said Joseph Jimenez, the former CEO of Novartis. "And not only does it have to be crystal clear, but everybody in the organization has to understand it, they have to have line of sight to that goal, and they have to understand how what they're doing is going to help us move into the future. You have to distill the strategy down to its essence for how we're going to win, and what we're really going to go after, so that people can hold it in their heads."

But that's not what companies typically share at all-hands meetings. Instead, leaders unveil strategy slides with, say, six bullet points alongside a tiered, colored pyramid, with maybe a corkscrew arrow or two thrown in for good measure. They may make sense in the moment, but if nobody can remember them, or if employees are not sure about how they're supposed to contribute to the strategy, then it is a wasted exercise. It is a fact of life that most people can't remember more than three or four things day to day. Given the complex messages that many chief executives push out to their employees, it would seem they don't appreciate the limitations of people's memories. In our work at Merryck with leadership teams, we often ask everyone in the group, in interviews before an off-site, to explain the company's strategy to us. More often than not, we hear very different answers from each person.

But effective leaders do understand the power of simplicity. That's why Bob Iger of Disney would find any excuse to remind people of the same top-three priorities for Disney that he had been evangelizing since his first day on the job. They were so central to Iger's leadership that they were listed in the second sentence of his bio on Disney's website: generating the best creative connect possible; fostering innovation and utilizing the latest technology; and expanding into new markets around the world. "You have to convey your priorities clearly and repeatedly," Iger writes in his autobiography, *The Ride of a Lifetime*. "If you don't articulate your priorities clearly, then the people around you don't know what their own should be. Time and energy and capital get wasted. You can do a lot for the morale of the people around you (and therefore the people around them) just by taking the guesswork out of their day-to-day life. A lot of work is complex and requires intense amounts of focus and energy, but this kind of messaging is fairly simple: This is where we want to be. This is how we're going to get there."

> "This is where we want to be. This is how we're going to get there."
>
> —Bob Iger, Executive Chairman, The Walt Disney Company

That drive to simplify is why McDonald's focused relentlessly in its early years on four areas: quality, cleanliness, service, and value (QCS&V). Ray Kroc, who built McDonald's from a local chain into a global enterprise, repeated it so often that he once said, "If I had a brick for every time I've repeated the phrase 'quality, service, cleanliness and value,' I think I'd probably be able to bridge the Atlantic Ocean with them."[1] When McDonald's leadership team updated its strategy in 2017, it developed a similarly simple mantra of "retain, regain and convert" as its growth strategy—to hold onto its best customers, win back the customers it had lost, and convert casual customers to more frequent ones.

That push for clarity is why, when Shawn Layden took over as chairman of Sony Interactive Entertainment Worldwide Studios in 2016, he came up with a three-part rubric for his global teams when they asked him about his plan. "I'm going to make it super simple," he said. "When you come up with game ideas and you want to propose something, just think of three things: first, best, and must. 'First' means, are you going to create a new game that has never been seen before, something completely innovative? 'Best' means, is the game you're proposing going to be the best in class? 'Must' means something we should do, like developing content to support the virtual-reality headsets that Sony created. If you have a game idea and it's not the first or it's not the best or it's not a must-do, then we're not going to do that game."

If simplifying complexity is a key skill for leaders, as the previous examples show, then how do you use that to develop a simple plan to align everybody around strategy? As much as we would like to be able to provide a handy worksheet with shortcuts for writing a simple plan, that approach won't work because the goal is to simplify complexity, not oversimplify it. That said, we can provide a conceptual framework to help you and your team develop a simple plan, and we can share some insights on how to avoid the pitfalls that we've seen time and again in working with leaders to develop them. This requires an investment of time to get your team aligned around shared goals, create a concise plan to achieve them, and develop a way to measure progress. Creating a simple plan is like setting the trajectory of a rocket launch; if you are even a few degrees off, over time you will miss your mark by a long shot. The process requires patience and time, but the patience will be rewarded with faster execution of your strategy. "When I came into the role, I had this gift of a nine-month transition before I took the helm officially, and I took the team through a strategy refresh," said Kelly Grier, Ernst & Young's US chairman and Managing Partner and Americas Managing Partner. "We deliberated every decision, and we analyzed and debated every data set. Ultimately, we landed on a common vision. The trust we built because of the honest conversations and this commitment to think more holistically drove a different mindset."

So how do you develop a simple plan? We'll repeat our caveat that this idea, like many others in this book, is meant to start a productive conversation with your team, rather than provide the final word on the topic. We also want to acknowledge that others have created frameworks worth considering that aim to achieve the same goal of simplification and alignment. Greg Brenneman, the chairman of private equity firm CCMP Capital, who has a long career of implementing turnaround strategies at companies that include Continental Airlines, Quiznos, Burger King, and PwC Consulting, uses a one-page approach that he developed for analyzing companies he's considering joining or buying. He divides a sheet of paper into four columns—labeled market, financial, product, and people—and then writes down the key actions that the company could take in each area to improve its prospects. "If I couldn't write that one-page plan or had trouble identifying the key value levers, then I knew pretty quickly that the company would be better off in someone else's hands," Brenneman writes in his book, *Right Away & All at Once*. Intel created an approach called OKRs, for objectives and key results, that has been widely adopted by some companies, Google among them.

Salesforce's Marc Benioff created his V2MOM framework—vision, values, methods, obstacles, and measures—for aligning everyone at his company around a shared goal.

All these approaches have merit, though we have found in our experience of working with senior leaders and their teams that words like "mission" and "vision" often have the same Rorschach-test effect as the word "strategy." They can mean different things to different people and often lead to existential conversations about meaning and purpose that can distract from the task at hand, which is to develop a clear and simple plan *to grow the company.*

We have found the most useful framework is an approach that Dinesh Paliwal, the former CEO of Harman International, developed. He said, "When we go to our board now, every business strategy is described in one page, with simple messaging. What is the goal, the core message, in one line? What are the three key actions we're taking? What are the three key challenges? And how do we measure success in twelve months? My board members read that, and it's much easier for them to understand. Simplifying the message is not just an art. It is a practice, and it doesn't happen in one day. It doesn't come naturally to most of us. It's work and you have to spend time on it."

Let's take a closer look at each of the elements in Paliwal's model, which leaders at all levels can use to clarify the goals and strategies for their particular team, business unit, or division.

The core message, in one line, is the answer to Kevin's "what's the big idea?" question. This isn't about what you're going to work on, or a description of the business or general direction, but rather what you are setting out to achieve. In our work with teams, we find that switching contexts helps focus the discussion. Imagine you're trying to raise money from a group of skeptical investors (think *Shark Tank*). Or that you're preparing a five-minute, three-slide presentation to your impatient board of directors who want to know, "What are you doing with all the resources we're giving you?" Or what if you were trying to recruit a top prospect in your industry who was choosing among five great job offers from all your biggest competitors, and you had to make a case that is both ambitious and specific for why that person should join your team? How do you plan to win?

An example of that kind of big idea can be found in a 2015 document published by the New York Times Company. At the time, the company's prospects seemed grim. Revenue from print advertising, the foundation of its business for decades, was falling quickly, and revenue from digital advertising and digital subscriptions was growing slowly. The leadership team set an ambitious target: "We are setting the goal of doubling our digital revenues over the next five years, to reach more than $800 million in digital-only revenue by 2020. To get there, we must more than double the number of engaged digital readers who are the foundation of both our consumer and advertising revenue models."[2] That's the big idea—the what, the why, and a glimpse of the how, all packed into two sentences.

With a clear goal like that serving as the compass, it's time to start filling in the map of how you're going to get there. What are the big levers you're going to pull to achieve that goal? There can't be ten. There probably should be no more than three or four, and they shouldn't include obligatory mentions of all the work you're doing already. Where are you going to apply resources with greater intensity and focus? At the Times, those levers included building its international audience, growing digital advertising by creating more compelling and integrated ad experiences for which they could charge a premium, and improving the customer experience for its readers.

Once you've articulated the levers you're going to pull to reach the big goal, then your organization chart should reflect those initiatives, with top talent assigned to each of them. Don Gogel, chairman of the private equity firm Clayton, Dubilier & Rice, would regularly bring up this point in strategy review sessions with companies in CD&R's portfolio. "One of the most important questions is whether the best people are working on the most critical projects," Gogel said. "We'll start that discussion by asking, What are the company's top five priorities? Who's staffing them and to whom do they report? Companies very often will give those top-priority projects to people a few levels down in the organization because they have some time available. But if these really are the most important projects, you've got to put your best people on them. Otherwise, you're giving mixed signals to the organization. Ensuring that top talent is working on key organizational priorities is essential, and most companies simply overlook this fundamental fact."

After the three or four big goals have been articulated, then it's equally important to be clear on the challenges that the company is facing. This can be hard for some executives because they would rather be inspirational cheerleaders, even though the troops are fully aware of the headwinds. The Times Company had its truth-telling moment in 2014, when an internal newsroom document called the "Innovation Report," which was intended for a small audience of leaders in the company, was leaked to and published for public consumption by BuzzFeed. The unvarnished language in the report (Adam was a member of the newsroom team that researched and wrote the document) chronicled the Times's many challenges at the time, including its siloed culture, an outsized and outdated focus on the print paper and website home page, and the slow adoption of the audience-building tactics that BuzzFeed, the *Huffington Post*, and other sites were using more effectively. There are less painful and public ways than a leaked internal report to achieve the same effect, of course—the leadership team instead can acknowledge internally the challenges the company faces—but the goal is to create a shared understanding of the difficulties that lie ahead.

Finally, you need a way to measure progress. What's the scoreboard? At the Times Company, the key measure was tracking the growth of digital subscriptions, given that so much of its business flows from that single metric (more loyal readers attract more advertisers). We'll share more on the Times as a case study of digital transformation in chapter 4, but note here that the company has executed its simple plan, passing its $800 million goal for digital revenue ahead of schedule.

Is the example of the Times Company easily transferable to other companies and industries? Of course not. The urgency to find a new direction, because its traditional business model was unsustainable, is not shared by established multinational companies with big portfolios of businesses in different industries, or by companies with strategies that are largely working already. But this is why simplifying complexity is such a crucial test. Developing a simple plan to galvanize the organization and build energy toward shared goals is a leader's job. Get it right and everyone will feel aligned to win in the marketplace. They will have a clear compass and will feel empowered to draw the map. But miss the mark and you will have created a fuzzy document that creates little clarity, and people will then just focus on their own jobs with little sense of how their work connects to a broader goal.

In our work with leadership teams, we have seen some common challenges that arise when they start developing a simple plan, so keep the following tips in mind as you're working on yours.

Focus on Outcomes, Rather Than Priorities

Rather than framing the discussion around the question "What are we going to work on?" ask yourself, "What do we need to accomplish? What are the three or four things that, if we accomplish them over the next twelve months, will make this a good year?" This is the approach that John Donahoe, the CEO of Nike, uses with his leadership teams. "Priorities for priorities' sake are dangerous," he said. "Priorities have to be geared to a specific outcome in mind. And they have to be measurable, but they don't always have to be quantitative. I might write statements that I want to be able to say yes to at the end of the year. It might be about launching one or two new products for the next year. There might not be metrics for everything, but the question is, have we achieved that outcome, and can we identify the specifics that we need to tackle to achieve it?"

Ron Williams, the former CEO of Aetna, used a clever metaphor to help his team think about the planning process in a way that focused them on specific outcomes. He said:

The simple way I explain strategy to people is that it's like having a time machine. You get in your time machine, and you go forward five years. You get out, and you observe very carefully everything that's going on. Who is winning? Why are they winning? What's going on? You get in your time machine, and you come back. Your strategy is a bridge to the future. That helps with alignment. It provides great clarity to the organization because they have a sense of how you define reality and a sense of where you're taking the organization, which helps with hope and aspiration because the vision you have painted is vivid and clear. When you create a very structured alignment, then you can get this whole ship moving through the water at a very good speed. The purpose of the plan and the strategy isn't because the world is going to unfold exactly the way you think it is. The point is that when it doesn't, you know exactly what to change and what to do.

Williams's time-machine metaphor also raises an important consideration: you have to decide up front about the time horizon of your plan. A one-year plan may make more sense for a startup, while a three- to five-year plan will better suit a large and more established company.

Edit Ruthlessly

The simple plan is not an exercise in giving space to everyone's hobby horse. The goal is a succinct summary of the actions that the top team will own. What are the areas that are going to get new or greater focus to achieve the outcome? Check the verbs in your document. If a bullet point starts with "continuing to" or similar language, it shouldn't be on the list, because presumably that item is what your company should be doing at all times.

Prune out flowery adjectives and jargon, too, applying the test that Susan Salka, the CEO of AMN Healthcare, a staffing company, learned from her father. She said:

"Can you create a vision that the frontline person can understand, and see how they fit into it?"

—Susan Salka, CEO, AMN Healthcare

One of his expressions had to do with keeping things simple and making people feel comfortable around you. If somebody was talking over his head, using big words, being too complex, or trying to act too sophisticated, he would say, "Would you break that down to cows, chickens, and taters?" I used to think it was silly—what do cows, chickens and taters have to do with each other? But years later, I realized that the message is, keep it simple. Don't overcomplicate things. As a leader, that's something that I've really learned over time. The strategy and the business can be complex, but you have to explain them in a way that's really easy to understand. Can you create a vision that the frontline person can understand, and see how they fit into it?

Make Yourself Uncomfortable

One inherent challenge in developing a simple plan is that, when done right, it introduces career risk. It is much easier to frame a simple plan in the spirit of "priorities we will continue to work on," without specific outcomes or targets in mind, thereby guaranteeing success. The simple plan should be ambitious enough to prompt a collective "can we really get there?" gulp by the team, with compensation plans aligned with the simple plan to incentivize the team to reach the shared goals. The leader's job is to set a high bar, but even the most senior executives can have their personal reasons for not wanting to set it too high. They may have worked long and hard to get their current job and would like to enjoy it for a while, so they adopt an approach that is more about making tweaks at the margins to muddle through—the business equivalent of the physician's oath to first do no harm. "I remember telling one CEO that I don't want to hear any more that 'It's about the journey,'" said Chris Brody the former Warburg Pincus partner. "I'd like to know what the destination is."

Beware of "Expert-itis"

People can get so deeply immersed in their field, with a keen appreciation of subtle nuances, that they find it hard to pull themselves back to a distance from which they can see the forest for the trees. What seems obvious to them is not obvious to everyone else, so they dismiss the elements of a simple plan as truisms that everyone knows and believes in—"It's like motherhood and apple pie," said one leader we worked with of the exercise. Instead, they dive deeply into more granular, internally focused matters like decision rights and budgets around initiatives for the next quarter, rather than on the big levers that should be pulled to win in the marketplace. A hallmark of effective simple plans is that they may seem obvious, like Iger's three-part strategy for driving the company. "Well, of course," you might say. "What else would it be?" But the fact is that his three-part plan has been the driving force of Disney's long track record of growth, and a key reason for Iger's success in that role. Another reason people can get lost in expert-itis is that there is a sense of job security in complexity, as in, "I'm the only person who really gets how complicated this is, so the company can't live without me." It's the leader's job to capture the essence of what matters. "If you ask CEOs 'What's important?' a lot of them will give you twenty-one single-spaced pages of their priorities," said Brenneman of CCMP. "And that's not going to work. What is your one-page plan?"

Test It

How do you know when you have it right? After you and your leadership team have developed a simple plan, then it's time to start pressure-testing it with key focus groups, including employees and, if you're the CEO, perhaps key directors, since the board ultimately will need to agree to the approach. What's clear? What's not clear? What's missing? Do employees understand how their jobs fit into the plan? Do they understand what they should focus on day to day and why it's important? Are they clear on the scoreboard for measuring progress? Is the strategy memorable enough to pass the hallway test—if you stopped a dozen employees randomly as they were walking between meetings and asked them to articulate the strategy, would you hear the same answer, or twelve different ones? And the plan should be the same for all your key audiences, including employees, directors, customers, and investors.

> ## "If you ask CEOs 'What's important?' a lot of them will give you twenty-one single-spaced pages of their priorities."
> **—Greg Brenneman, Executive Chairman, CCMP Capital**

Let's say you've done all the work we've described, and you have your simple plan. It's crisp and clear, and everyone is eager to link arms and start working. Congratulations. As the leader, you are now halfway there.

Now you need to live a key principle of leadership: there is no such thing as overcommunication. You have to repeat the simple plan relentlessly, no matter how redundant the messaging may feel to you. "At first I wondered how many times I'd have to say the same thing," said Andi Owen, chief executive of Herman Miller, the office furniture company. "Then I realized that there are eight thousand employees, and in almost every venue I'm in, people are meeting me for the first time. I have to repeat the core message over and over because my job is to set the direction, communicate, and be inspiring. I thought I would spend a lot more time doing some other things, but most of my day is spent communicating."

Owen's insight was echoed by Christopher Nassetta, the CEO of Hilton Worldwide. "You have to be careful as a leader, particularly of a big organization," he said. "You can find yourself communicating the same thing so many times that you get tired of hearing it. And so you might alter how you say it, or shorthand it, because you have literally said it so many times that you think nobody else on earth could want to hear this. But you can't stop. In my case, there are 420,000 people who need to hear it, and I can't say it enough. So what might sound mundane and like old news to me isn't for a lot of other people. That is an important lesson I learned as I worked in bigger organizations."

The need to constantly remind people of the strategy can seem puzzling. After all, people are smart, and presumably they can remember the key components of a simple plan from week to week. One answer is captured in an insight from Marcus Ryu, the chairman and cofounder of Guidewire, which makes software for the insurance industry. "I've come to realize that no matter how smart the people are who you're communicating to, the more of them there are, the dumber the collective gets. And so you could have a room full of Einsteins, but if there are two hundred or three hundred of them, then you still have to talk to them like they're just average people. As the audience gets bigger and bigger, your message has to get simpler and simpler, and the bullet-point list has to be shorter and shorter."

"Never give people a void. Just don't, because instinctively they'll think something is awry."

—Geoff Vuleta, founding CEO, A King's Ransom

A second reason why repetition is so important is captured in this warning from Geoff Vuleta, the CEO at A King's Ransom, a consulting firm: "Never give people a void. Just don't, because instinctively they'll think something is awry." Businesses, just as in nature, abhor a vacuum, and if leaders aren't saying anything, then employees will supply their own narrative, and they will often go to a dark place, spinning conspiracies or worst-case scenarios. Uncertainty creates free-floating, contagious anxiety.

"People read a lot more meaning into things that you didn't necessarily intend to have meaning," said Christy Wyatt, the CEO of Absolute Software, a cybersecurity company. "People will make up stories in the white space." One vivid reminder of this rule played out when she was leading another firm called Good Technology. Like most Silicon Valley companies, it had a kitchen stocked with free snacks and drinks. The company decided to switch the vendors that supplied the snacks, so there was a week when supplies ran low before the new vendor took over. "Because we hadn't said anything about it, and the food was starting to run low, people started saying, 'There's layoffs coming; bad things are going to happen,'" Wyatt recalled. "I actually had to say in an all-hands meeting, 'Guys, it's just the nuts in the kitchen. That's it.' But people look for symbols, and they look for meaning where maybe there isn't any. So now we're overcommunicating. You have to talk about the little stuff as well as the big stuff, just to make sure folks aren't running away with ideas."

Tom Lawson, the CEO of FM Global, a property insurance company, learned a similar lesson when he oversaw the company's research group. He had one particularly rough morning when he was late for work, it was raining, and he got soaked running through the parking lot to join a conference call. He walked right past the receptionist, went into his office, and shut the door. About three hours later, his head of research knocked and said, "We've got a problem. Everyone's talking that the company's in financial trouble and that our research is going to get outsourced." Lawson was stunned and asked why. "You walked right into the building on the day we released our financials and you didn't talk to anybody," his colleague said. "You shut your door and you locked yourself in here." In fact, the company's financials were fine, but it was a lesson to Lawson about how actions can be misinterpreted. "Everybody's paying attention all the time, and so it's not just what you say; it's how you act," he said. "If you don't communicate, people will make up narratives themselves, and they may be negative."

Finally, prepare to be teased for endlessly repeating the strategy. If your employees roll their eyes and say what you're going to say before you open your mouth, consider that a victory because they have internalized the message. Getting to that point requires far more communication than you might think, and in all forms—all-hands meetings, email blasts, webcasts. All these approaches are necessary to fight the collective short attention spans in organizations.

"You tell people, 'Here's where we're headed and these are our priorities,' and then you just sense how often people are wandering," said Laurel Richie, the former president of the Women's National Basketball Association. "I always say that part of the job is keeping all the bunnies in the box. You start with all the bunnies in the box and then somebody gets a great idea to go do something else and you go help them all come back and get in line and then a bunny over here pops out. So the more the bunnies are getting out of the box, the more I realize I just haven't done a good enough job communicating what our priorities are and what our focus should be."

All leaders have their blind spots, those disconnects between how they think they are showing up in the world and how their employees perceive them (and in this context, perception is reality). One of the biggest disconnects arises around this question of strategy. What is clear and simple in the leader's head is often not as clear and simple to everyone else. Because of the powerful gravitational pull in business to make things more complicated than they are or than they should be, a leader's job is to provide the counterweight of a relentless drive to simplify complexity, and to develop a jargon-free plan for winning that everyone understands, remembers, and knows how to contribute to its success. The simple plan will evolve over time, of course, based on new insights from the results of various initiatives. But the point is to start with a clear plan so you know what to adjust and why when market conditions change.

> ## "I always say that part of the job is keeping all the bunnies in the box."
> **—Laurel Richie, former President, WNBA**

Kevin's question—"What's the big idea, and so what?"—is effective shorthand to start building the habit inside your company of simplifying complexity and designing a simple plan to ensure everyone is aligned around a clear goal, the levers to achieve it, the challenges that stand in your way, and the scoreboard for measuring progress.

Test #2
Can You Make the Culture Real— and Matter?

It's about walking the talk.

Corporate culture can be messy and maddening.

To start, there are mixed views on the importance of culture. Given that it doesn't show up anywhere on balance sheets or earnings statements, some would rather avoid discussing it altogether, impatient with its touchy-feely nature and more interested in what they can analyze in the columns and rows of a spreadsheet. At many companies, people view culture as little more than a checkbox exercise to develop a list of generic values that are posted in the "About us" section of the corporate website and rarely mentioned again.

The topic can also inspire eye rolls of cynicism, and for good reason. Every few months, it seems, another company is caught up in a scandal of its own making, and the diagnoses inevitably lead to problems of culture, including the Orwellian gap between the espoused values of the company and how employees, particularly the leaders, behaved. When Travis Kalanick was running Uber, a video circulated of him berating an Uber driver in a disagreement over pricing. "Some people don't like to take responsibility for their own [expletive]," Kalanick told the driver. "They blame everything in their life on somebody else."[1] At the time, "principled confrontation" was one of Uber's values.

Culture also can be a source of frustration for leaders, particularly because of their inability to influence and shape it unilaterally in an era when employees feel emboldened to speak up. Workers are demanding more, shifting the conversation to what employees can and should expect from their company, rather than vice versa. Silicon Valley companies led in encouraging people to bring their whole selves to work, and many employees have taken their companies' "obligation to dissent" invitations to heart, pressing for a say, often through social media channels, on everything from their company's stance on immigration laws to which products they should sell and to whom. Examples include the letter that thirty-one hundred Google employees signed and sent to CEO Sundar Pichai in 2018, protesting the company's work to develop AI technology for the military. "We believe that Google should not be in the business of war," they wrote. In early 2020, employees at Hachette Book Group walked out over the company's plan to publish Woody Allen's memoir, ultimately forcing the publisher's hand to pull back. And during the widespread protests over George Floyd's death, hundreds of Facebook employees staged a "virtual walkout" to protest their own company's hands-off approach to President Donald Trump's inflammatory posts. Leaders may applaud the ideals of democracy, but they probably don't expect that every key decision they make might be put to a vote.

Tempting as it may be for leaders to throw up their hands in frustration, building a strong culture is a leadership imperative, another crucial test that will determine whether they succeed. At its best, a strong culture can help with recruitment and retention, creating a kind of special club that people want to join and protect once they're part of it. Done right, culture will engage something deeper within employees' sense of themselves, ideally in ways that are aligned with business goals. "Culture is almost like a religion," said Robert L. Johnson, a cofounder of Black Entertainment Television. "People buy into it and they believe in it. And you can tolerate a little bit of heresy, but not a lot." Work becomes more of their identity—what they stand for, the contributions they want to make, what they aspire to be. But if there aren't clear and consistent guidelines for behavior, or if they are not reinforced and modeled every day by the top leaders, cultures can devolve into hives of dysfunction, insecurity, fear, and chaos. Instead of bringing out the best in people, they bring out the worst, as if somebody created a sport with no rules or referees on the field.

> "Culture is almost like a religion.
> People buy into it and they believe
> in it. And you can tolerate a little
> bit of heresy, but not a lot."
>
> —Robert L. Johnson, cofounder, BET

To be clear, there is no "right" company culture, in the same way that there is no "right" culture among all the countries in the world. A startup's culture is going to be different from the culture of a *Fortune* 100 company that's been around for 150 years. Creative firms are going to have more freewheeling cultures than companies in, say, health care, where people's lives are at stake. That said, there are some practices that come up time and again among leaders who are thoughtful about ensuring that the culture of their company matters. The practices include providing clarity around the behaviors leaders expect of employees based on the stated values, and reinforcing them at every opportunity, including quarterly and annual awards, in decisions to hire, promote, and fire people. Regular surveys of employees to ask them whether managers are behaving in accordance with the stated values are a must—without a rigorous process to determine what people are experiencing, leaders will be flying blind, relying only on anecdotes and assertions. Most important, the top leaders must own and model the values, so that there is no gap between what they say and what they do. When the culture feels more like a firm platform, rather than shifting sands beneath people's feet, employees are more likely to feel a sense of ownership of the culture.

To help bring these themes to life, we're going to share in detail the approach that one company—Twilio, a cloud communications company based in San Francisco—used to build its culture. Again, we're not suggesting its culture is more right than any others, but it does provide a rich example of how one company has tried to create a virtuous cycle of reinforcement to ensure all its employees understand and live its culture. Jeff Lawson, the CEO and a cofounder of Twilio, is particularly thoughtful about culture, and we'll be sharing the metaphorical microphone with him throughout this example to share his insights.

. . .

Lawson caught the entrepreneurial bug young. Growing up in Detroit, he started his first company when he was twelve, videotaping weddings, birthday parties, and bar mitzvahs. By the time he graduated from high school, he was making a few thousand dollars a weekend. In what little free time he had left during his teenage years, he also learned to code, writing computer programs for his friend's father's company, which provided software for industrial printers. Lawson credits his late grandfather as a big influence on his early work ethic. "Papa Vic," as he was known, ran his own paint business for forty years, but even after he sold it, he kept working well into his nineties, with others driving him on his rounds to sell paint accessories to retailers. "He did that job until literally the day he died," Lawson said. "The owner of every hardware store in Detroit came to the funeral. That was amazing."

At the University of Michigan, Lawson studied film and computer science, and started a couple of companies on the side, including Notes for Free. The company hired college students to transcribe class notes into a web-based system, then gave them away for free but made money by selling advertising on the site. Lawson raised some funding from investors to grow the business, and he dropped out of college during his senior year to work on the company full-time. Once the company had about fifty employees in Ann Arbor, it moved the entire staff to Silicon Valley in late 1999. Like many entrepreneurs, Lawson had little time or inclination to think much about culture in his first company, though he did learn that its haphazard feel was hurting its ability to hire more seasoned professionals. Lawson recalled:

> I think they were looking around and thinking, what the hell is going on here? We went nine months without being able to make a single hire for senior technical roles. I didn't think about it that much at the time because I was too inexperienced to realize it, but in retrospect, I realized that we just had not been intentional about the culture we were building, and it was just kind of a mess. Professionals saw a company that just had no kind of North Star, and no defined culture. It was just a bunch of people running around. That worked when we were a tech company in Michigan, but when you get out to

Silicon Valley, people know what a good culture looks like. When it isn't there, it's just not attractive. You don't know what you're joining.

Lawson sold Notes for Free to a competitor that had filed to go public, but because it was an equity deal, everyone's shares were soon wiped out in the dot-com crash.

"When I left Amazon, I had that understanding that culture is like an operating system."

—Jeff Lawson, cofounder and CEO, Twilio

Lawson then started two other companies before joining Amazon in 2004 as a technical product manager, a role that provided him a crash course in the importance of culture. Amazon is not for everyone—it has faced plenty of criticism over the years about its hard-driving culture—but there is no arguing that it has managed to make its leadership principles, including "invent and simplify," "bias for action," and "disagree and commit" part of everyday conversation in meetings. "We all walked around knowing and saying and using them every day," Lawson said. "They weren't just words on the wall. They weren't just rules about what you could and couldn't do, but they were trying to answer questions—How do we all be smarter? How do we get our jobs done together in a way that we can all understand what each other is saying? And how do we make good decisions? So when I left Amazon, I had that understanding that culture is like an operating system." Lawson, still in his late twenties, and his two cofounders, Evan Cooke and John Wolthuis, started Twilio roughly two years later, in January 2008, after hatching the idea in a coffee shop. Adding to their degree of difficulty, they launched the company into the teeth of the financial crisis, a tough time to try to raise money from investors. They borrowed money from family and friends to build what's called an MVP (minimum viable product). Lawson and his wife, Erica, even returned all the unopened gifts from her recent wedding shower to Bed Bath & Beyond to raise another $20,000.

Creating values is a rite of passage for companies, and there are many schools of thought on the right way, and the right time, to do the exercise. Some founders argue that the values should be written in the early days of forming a company to set a strong foundation; others believe some time should pass before starting the exercise to capture the culture after it evolves. Some believe the values should be lofty and aspirational, while others argue the values should be more prescriptive about the specific behaviors they want to encourage and discourage. Some argue that the value sets should be no longer than three or four to help people remember them, while others say the number doesn't matter all that much.

Lawson and his cofounders decided to wait on the values exercise for a few years, until the company had grown to about sixty employees. Lawson said:

Defining your culture is both an organic process and a very intentional one. The organic part of it is that you can't force a culture. You can do some thinking about who you are and who you want to be and what you really value, but it does take some time. I compare company building to growing up as a person. When you're a kid, you don't really know who you are yet. As a teenager, you're trying to figure it out and you go through different phases to see what feels right or wrong. And eventually, after all that process of discovery, you start to figure out who you are as an adult. Companies are the same way. We took a rough stab at our values in the early days, but we didn't hold on to them too religiously because we didn't really know who we were yet, and we were flexible enough to say let's keep learning about ourselves. When you get to around thirty to a hundred employees, that's when you really have to start to formalize the structures and the mechanisms of propagating the culture. Before then, you don't know what the culture is yet, and you're likely going to get it wrong, and if you're too adamant about those early values, it's just going to feel false. But if you wait too long, then you're likely to find yourself in really dangerous territory.

Lawson is careful to always use the word "articulation" to describe the act of writing a set of values. "You don't make them up," he said. "You can articulate what's already there and then put words to them, and the words are like handles. Because without handles, you could say, 'There's this thing I feel when I walk into work every day, but I don't know exactly what it is.' And once you give handles to talk about those important things, you can invoke them in a meeting and when you're making decisions. But if you don't have handles on them, they're just this amorphous thing, and they definitely risk getting diluted or disappearing. To me, articulating the values is the exercise of putting the best words possible to describe that feeling you have when you come to work."

At Twilio, the exercise of articulating the values started with Lawson enlisting a dozen employees who seemed the most invested in the idea of building a culture. He brought them together over a dinner and put the challenge to the group: "It's time that we articulate the values of the company—our job is to figure out what makes Twilio Twilio and put words to it." That brainstorm led to a list of about a hundred ideas. Lawson then did some work on the list himself, grouping the words into clusters that spoke to different ideas and sharpening some of the language. He brought the group back together twice more to help edit the new versions, and then presented them with a list of a dozen values for a final winnowing, asking each member of the group to vote on the ones that they thought were spot on and the ones they could live without. Lawson wanted the process to involve a key group of employees who would champion the values among their colleagues; he had them unveil the values at a company all-hands meeting. "It wasn't just Jeff walking down from the mountain with the tablets," Lawson said. That said, he also didn't think it should be a purely democratic process, with every employee getting an equal vote. "I'm the CEO and I'm a cofounder, and it's my job to get these right," Lawson said. "So I did take editorial control of the process and I also had the final say on the words we were going to use. I brought people along and I listened carefully to everyone's input, but ultimately it is the CEO's job. You can't outsource it to HR or do a companywide poll. It's your job to own the process."

While that early list included some phrases that you're likely to find on other companies' lists of values, including "Be humble" and "Empower others," there were two that stood out as unusual. One is "Draw the owl," based on the tongue-in-cheek internet meme that includes only two panels to explain how to draw an owl. The first panel shows three overlapping circles with the caption, "Step 1, draw some circles." The second panel shows a fully rendered owl over the words, "Step 2, draw the rest of the [expletive] owl." The pointed message is to jump right in and figure out things for yourself, rather than looking for a hundred-page, step-by-step instruction book. When the meme first appeared online, it went viral inside Twilio, and employees adopted it as a shorthand for the role of a startup.

> ## "We wanted to have words that would naturally come out of people's mouths, so that they would be accessible, memorable, and understandable."
>
> **—Jeff Lawson, cofounder and CEO, Twilio**

Another value is "No shenanigans." Lawson said he liked its clarity and conversational tone. "You know what shenanigans are and what they aren't," he added. "When you are engaging in shenanigans or when you see shenanigans, you know it. You can call it out and people understand that. We wanted to have words that would naturally come out of people's mouths, so that they would be accessible, memorable, and understandable. So we literally asked ourselves, could these be hashtags? Think about the defining attributes of hashtags. They're memorable, they're usable, you can throw them out in conversation, and everyone knows what they mean."

It's a point worth emphasizing. If you think of two of the biggest and most successful companies—Amazon and Microsoft—each of them is known for a single phrase that defines their culture and could be hashtags. Jeff Bezos, the founder of Amazon, has long evangelized the idea of "Day 1" thinking to remind employees to approach their work every day as if they were building a startup and not get caught in the "because we've always done it that way" trap that can slow down innovation at large companies. At Microsoft, Satya Nadella has challenged the company to move from a culture of "know it alls" to a culture of "learn it alls," crystallizing the ideas of fixed-versus-growth mindsets that he learned about from Angela Duckworth, the author of *Grit: The Power of Passion and Perseverance*. Another example is Novartis, which has embraced the thinking of Lars Kolind, a Danish entrepreneur and author who wrote *Unboss*. Its simple point is that teams are best positioned to come up with solutions, so the leader's job is to support them rather than telling them what to do. "If we had chosen 'empowered,' nobody would have asked a question about it," said Steven Baert, the chief people and organization officer at Novartis. "Everybody would say, 'I get it.' But now people are more likely to ask, 'What exactly do you mean by "unbossed"?' That in and of itself is a gift, because people want to discuss it, which helps create a change platform."

After drawing up that original list of nine values, the team at Twilio later wrote a second list of eight leadership principles. Lawson recognized the risk of having two long lists but believed that the team created a broad and useful set of tools. "The question was always whether you'd rather have fewer of these things, because the fewer words you use, the more impactful they each are." he said. "Or do you want to have a longer list because you can decide which principle is most relevant at a particular moment in time?" In 2018, Twilio acquired another company, SendGrid, which added about a third more people to the company. SendGrid had its own four values of hungry, happy, honest, and humble. "It seemed like the perfect time to say, let us take this moment to rearticulate our values," Lawson said.

That prompted a companywide exercise to refresh the values and included visits by Lawson and other senior executives to its twenty offices worldwide to conduct an exercise with each group. They wrote the seventeen Twilio values and leadership principles on note-cards and stuck them to a big whiteboard, and then gave everyone six stickers—three red and three blue. They told the groups to put a red sticker on the values that resonated most with them (red is the color that Twilio uses in all its branding) and a blue sticker on the ones that resonated the least with them. A clear pattern emerged. Some drew a lot of positive votes, others got a lot of "no" votes, and some had no stickers at all. Lawson said:

> The most interesting ones were half red, half blue. Some peo-
> ple loved them, some people said we should get rid of them,
> and those are the ones we spent time discussing as a group.
> A lot of the values meant different things to different people

based on when they joined and based on the quality of how we evangelized the values. Some people had joined the company a while ago, back when I was personally giving an hour-long talk to new hires about the values. There was a period when someone else did it, so people walked away with different ideas about what these values meant. Based on that, we went through an exercise of saying, how do we take the essence of what we want the values to represent in our culture and how do we get them into a set of words that get closer to how we would describe it?

The company came up with a refreshed list of ten values, organized into three categories:

How we act

Be an owner. Owners know their business, embracing the good news and the bad. Owners sweat the details and "pick up the trash." Owners think long term and spend money wisely.

Empower others. We believe that unleashing human potential—both inside and outside our company—is the key to our success. Be humble and realize it's not just about us. Invest in each other.

No shenanigans. Always act in an honest, direct, and transparent way.

How we make decisions

Wear the customer's shoes. Spend the time to deeply understand customers and solve problems from their perspective. Earn trust through every interaction.

Write it down. Our business is complex, so take the time to express yourself in prose—for your sake, and for the folks with whom you're collaborating.

Ruthlessly prioritize. Prioritization helps break down complex problems and provides clarity in the face of uncertainty. Decisions are progress, so make decisions with available information and keep learning.

How we win

Be bold. We're driven by a hunger to build a meaningful and impactful company. Embrace crazy ideas, and remember, every big idea starts small.

Be inclusive. To achieve our goals, we need a diverse set of voices in the room. Build diverse teams and seek out unique points of view.

Draw the owl. There's no instruction book; it's ours to write. Figure it out, ship it, and iterate. Invent the future, but don't wing it.

Don't settle. Expect the best from yourself and others, because there's no feeling greater than being proud of our work. Hire the best people for every role.

While there is an art form to developing a list of values—ideally, it should include input from people throughout the organization, and the values should be translatable into expected behaviors—the actual words are less important than whether top leaders model them and continually reinforce and bring them to life to show everyone that they matter. And yes, we are focusing far more on those behaviors in this chapter than the mission and vision statements that companies draw up. Those are laudable exercises, and such statements can provide a North Star for what the company does and why it matters (ideally, they should not strain credulity, like WeWork's "Our mission is to elevate the world's consciousness"). But we believe that a company's values, and the specific behaviors they are meant to promote, carry far more weight in the life of an organization because they help answer the seemingly simple questions that often are so challenging for leaders to answer: "What are we trying to accomplish as a company? What are we going to focus on to achieve that goal? How are we going to work together?" The simple plan framework that we described in the first chapter is designed to help sharpen the focus on answering the first two questions, and the values exercise is meant to help answer the third one.

Once companies develop their values and the expected behaviors, they have to be woven into the fabric of everyday life. At Twilio, for example, that starts with the hiring process. Lawson said that because one of its core values is "draw the owl," he tries to hire people who have demonstrated track records of creating things. "I'm looking for people who exhibit that builder mentality," he said. "So I'll ask, 'Tell me about something you've invented. It could be in your professional or personal life.' If they can't answer that question, that means they don't think of themselves as a builder, because people who think of themselves as a builder have pride in things they have invented." Once they're hired, Lawson or another member of the executive team will share, during the onboarding process, the backstories behind the values—how they came about, what they mean, what they look like in action, and why they're important.

The values are also reinforced through stories, creating culture heroes whose behavior is celebrated at quarterly and annual awards. Each year, for example, Twilio hands out "Superb Owl" awards to employees who have been role models for the values. (The Superb Owl award is an inside joke: owls are Twilio's mascot, the Super Bowl is a big day for many of its customers, and somebody pointed out that if you move the letter *b*, Super Bowl becomes Superb Owl.) The company considers whether an employee is embodying the values for their performance reviews and decisions about whether to promote somebody. It also asks employees in twice-a-year engagement surveys whether they feel that the company is living the stated values. But the most important test is this: Do employees at all levels use them in everyday conversation to help make decisions? Lawson said people often refer to, say, a roadblock that a team got around by drawing the owl. Or that they chose a particular path because the other options they were considering felt a bit more like shenanigans.

"When you hear those words being used all day long, that's when you know the values are real," he said.

Twilio's culture is by no means a finished work. Christy Lake, Twilio's chief people officer, who joined the company in early 2020 after working at companies such as Box, Medallia, HP, and Home Depot, said she would like to see a leadership curriculum built around each of the values. "What matters is whether the values live," she said. "Do they breathe? Are they part of your ethos and your DNA? Are they brought to life in behaviors, observable actions, how you communicate, and the behaviors you celebrate? That is what differentiates an amazing culture from a terrible culture. The second people see a shadow between the stated culture and how people behave, people will spot it and then you don't have a system. You're dead in the water."

> **"The second people see a shadow between the stated culture and how people behave, people will spot it and then you don't have a system."**
>
> **—Christy Lake, Chief People Officer, Twilio**

The company, by its own admission, is not where it wants to be in terms of diversity. It has published its goals on its website: to have women make up half its workforce by 2023 (up from 33 percent as of early 2020), and to have underrepresented populations make up

30 percent of its US workforce (up from 21 percent in early 2020). It also uses employee survey data to construct a "belonging and diversity index" and breaks out the results by gender and underrepresented populations. Its goal is to score 100 percent on that index globally, with the same score across the board for different groups. In the meantime, it has already built a leadership team that is far more diverse than most, and includes Black, Asian, and East Indian executives. When we wrote this, it had more women on the team (six) than white men (four). That is not something you see every day.

Perhaps it should go without saying that diversity and inclusion are fundamental to creating a strong culture. But just in case, a quick reminder: to solve problems and spot opportunities faster and more creatively, you need people with different perspectives, backgrounds, and thought processes around the table. As demographic trends create a more diverse world, you need leaders who reflect the customers you have and want. As businesses compete more intensely for talent, you need to draw from the biggest talent pool possible. Companies spend a lot of money and effort recruiting diverse workers, but they often don't stick around because the culture tolerates behaviors that make those employees feel unwelcome. Delivering on your promises of building a culture that values diversity and leadership will help you recruit and retain the best talent and avoid the cynicism that can creep into companies that don't back up their words with actions. Society is demanding more from companies, rewarding those with good reputations and penalizing those with bad ones.

While few leaders will argue these points, many companies are still falling short of their stated aspirations, repeating the same mantra on diversity that they have used for years: "We're not where we want to be on this issue, but we're committed to it and we're making progress." Their annual diversity reports may show small improvements in companywide numbers, but you likely will still see leadership teams that are overwhelmingly white and male, with a few executives who add some diversity to the group in staff roles like HR, marketing, and communications that do not carry P&L responsibilities.

The momentum for change is growing. In the wake of the killing of George Floyd by Minneapolis police officers in May 2020, there has been a sustained and heightened awareness of racism and social injustice in the United States, with an array of companies pledging to build a more diverse staff and to create more inclusive cultures. Many have said they will write large checks to nonprofits that work to address social injustice. But only a small subset of that group has made commitments to increase Black representation in their ranks of senior leaders. Until that changes, many of the pledges that companies are making, and the checks they are writing, will amount to little more than "placebo paternalism" as Robert Johnson, the BET cofounder, calls it.

Racism, diversity, and inclusion are deeply complex and multi-layered issues, and we don't want to suggest we have any new answers. But we do want to shine a bright spotlight on what can and should be done to increase representation of Black executives and other minorities in the C-suite and the one or two levels below. Board directors and their CEOs together must establish diversity and inclusion as a concrete goal that is on par, in terms of importance, with delivering financial returns, developing new products, and improving competitiveness on key measures. Part of the leader's bonus should depend on making progress on diversity and inclusion, and the metrics for performance should be based on achieving actual outcomes, not simply around activity. And they should include building a C-suite team with diverse leaders in roles with P&L responsibilities, not just in staff roles.

To help build the pipeline of Black leaders in the firms that Johnson owns through The RLJ Companies, he established a rule that was modeled after the National Football League's "Rooney Rule," which requires teams to interview minority candidates for head coaching and general manager roles. At his companies, anyone hiring at the director level or above must interview at least two Black candidates for the position. "They don't have to hire them," Johnson said. "It is a mandate to interview, because if the person wasn't right for that job, you keep their name in your system and they may be right for the next job. And if you do hire a minority candidate, then you're opening the door for other people to be considered because of their personal network. Once you get more people being considered, you will see more diversity in the people actually getting hired. And you do that at every level of the company, even when recruiting board directors, and people are held accountable by making part of their compensation based on meeting these goals."

. . .

The example of Twilio provides many key insights for creating and fostering an effective culture, including its stated and measurable commitment to increasing diversity in its workforce. But the build-from-scratch experience of a founder CEO like Jeff Lawson is not shared widely by other leaders. For example, what should a CEO do when they are hired to run an existing company, and they discover that the culture they are inheriting is troubled, where behaviors that directly contradict the espoused values are tolerated and even rewarded? Whenever an organization appoints a new leader, it is expecting some degree of change, and the leader must take full and quick advantage of it by using many of the same tools that Lawson used at Twilio. That includes a tough conversation with the senior team explaining that everyone, without exception, will be expected to model the behaviors that the values describe (dismissing a serial offender or two from the most senior ranks will send an immediate and uncompromising signal to the entire company). The leader can commission a task force of up-and-coming executives to revisit and potentially refresh the values. And they can establish a more sophisticated system for surveying employees' opinions on the culture and taking quick action on some of their feedback to show employees that they are being heard.

Leaders who are not the CEO face a much bigger challenge if they find themselves working in a dysfunctional culture, because they do not have access to all the levers that chief executives have to make sweeping changes. In such instances, leaders may default to a more passive role in the culture, arguing that the tone is set at the top and therefore beyond their control. They may even throw up their hands and complain about "this place," blaming an amorphous "them" for any shortcomings in the culture. In our consulting work, we have met many senior leaders who pride themselves on their sophisticated diagnoses of what is wrong with their own company's culture. Somehow, they fail to realize that, as leaders themselves, they have a responsibility to help build the culture rather than critique it. Whether they want to admit it or not, they are part of the "them" that they are complaining about. Leaders at all levels can play a role. Within their own teams and spheres of control, they can make clear the behaviors they expect their colleagues to live by, and to ensure that they themselves are doing the same. It is, in many ways, a matter of mindset. All employees, particularly leaders, must decide whether they are going to own their share of responsibility for building the culture—in effect, are they drivers or riders?

> **"If you're an employee, you don't write a review of the company, just like you don't write a review of being an American."**
> **—Marcus Ryu, cofounder and Chairman, Guidewire**

This distinction was captured in a smart metaphor from Marcus Ryu of Guidewire. He shared the story of a memo that he wrote to his employees, prompted by some feedback he read about the company on Glassdoor, a website where current and former employees can post anonymous reviews of their employers. Guidewire gets high marks overall, but Ryu found himself annoyed by some of

59

the posts—not because he was thin-skinned, but because he had a philosophical problem with the notion of employees critiquing their own company's culture for all the world to see. Ryu said:

> You write reviews when you are a consumer. If you stay at a hotel and you had a good or bad experience, then you can go to Tripadvisor and write a review. If you buy a product and you don't like it, you write a review on Amazon. But if you're an employee, you don't write a review of the company, just like you don't write a review of being an American. You are a citizen of this country. You can be critical of it, but your responsibilities as a citizen are not discharged by writing a review. That's completely the wrong paradigm. You don't consume your citizenship. You are a citizen. And what a citizen says is, "I want to belong to this collectivity because I believe in its principles. I want it to succeed, and therefore I have a duty." Citizenship has certain duties, and one of those duties is that this organization continues to thrive.

If you agree with Ryu's logic, then the test for all leaders is this: Can you create, and contribute to building, a culture that people will want to own as citizens? That will require a commitment to these foundational principles:

- Culture is the responsibility of the CEO and senior leaders to define, model, enforce and assess. They must continually talk about the culture and celebrate heroes who embody the values. Leaders must be evaluated on the degree to which they model the culture.

- Culture should be articulated through values and expected behaviors, and reviewed on occasion to ensure they remain appropriate to the times and current business circumstances of the company.

- Unrepentant "culture felons" who consistently behave in ways that directly contradict the stated values must be ushered out, regardless of their business performance, to send a clear signal that the company is serious about living the values.

- Perceptions of the culture among employees must be measured through periodic all-staff anonymous surveys to ensure that the day-to-day reality matches the aspiration. Anecdotes and assertions to describe the culture are inadequate and often misleading. Board directors must closely monitor those measurements of cultural health to ensure they are getting an accurate picture.

These are the enduring truths of how high-performing organizations approach culture. And while every company's culture will be different, they can help start the playbook that every organization should write for itself.

Test #3
Can You Build Teams That Are True Teams?

They are the key to driving the strategy.

At the age of twenty-seven, after passing a battery of navy exams, Kevin (one of the authors) was appointed new-construction engineer officer of the *USS Memphis*, a Los Angeles–class nuclear submarine that was the most advanced attack submarine at the time (a similar sub, the *USS Dallas*, was featured in the 1990 blockbuster *The Hunt for Red October*). When he showed up at the Newport News shipyard in Virginia, the sub was just a hull, and for the next two years, the $1 billion project was going to be his life. Kevin was responsible for managing a staff of one hundred, partnering with the shipyard, testing the sub's nuclear reactor plant, and training the crew to go to sea. Kevin wasn't new to management—he had been in charge of operations and maintenance for an engineering group on his prior submarine, with twenty-five men reporting to him. But this assignment was daunting because every aspect of it was a new challenge. He was under constant scrutiny, and the level of micromanagement he faced from day one was overwhelming. That pressure led him to adopt the same style with his own team—he once woke up a petty officer to remind him of a technical detail about the seals in a hydraulic plant—but he was so demanding and directive that he began to alienate his team, and the sub's captain counseled him that he had to find a new way. So Kevin shifted his approach, spending more time to ensure that everyone was crystal clear about their responsibilities, that they understood how he would measure progress, and then letting them do their work. Two years later, they delivered the submarine on time and on budget. "I figured out how to manage a team in a way that gave them the support they needed," he says. "We all had agreement on what good would look like. We had a high degree of trust. I could spend my time on the issues that needed focus, as opposed to trying to do everybody else's job."

Fourteen years later, after stints at AT&T, McKinsey, and General Electric, Kevin joined MCI as an executive vice president and learned over the next three years what it felt like to be part of a dysfunctional team. With its ambitious goal of being the telecom industry's David to take on the Goliath of AT&T, MCI was a freewheeling Wild West–style organization, a sharp contrast to the more disciplined leadership that Kevin had experienced in the navy and at GE. The leaders at MCI believed that disharmony and internal competition would bring out everybody's best work. The politics were all-consuming, and open warfare among the different groups was tolerated in the take-no-prisoners culture. Humiliating people was routine, like the time a senior executive berated one of Kevin's direct reports in front of him. "It was almost the complete anti-team," Kevin recalls. "It was an incredibly toxic brew of behaviors. Some could succeed despite this environment, but I was miserable at a level that I had never been before or since. I couldn't sleep. I could not focus or deliver. My hair was falling out. Those three years were the worst three years of my life, but they were the most important three years because I saw and felt, in sharp relief, what bad looked like."

He then joined Amgen as president, where he worked as second in command to CEO Gordon Binder for more than seven years. He wasn't given any guarantees that he eventually would become chief executive, but he was given a seat on the board, providing him an insider's edge over others who were competing to eventually take over from Binder. Eight years later, when he became CEO, Kevin could build the team he wanted. Over the next eighteen months, he recruited a new group of direct reports from companies such as Disney, Merck, GlaxoSmithKline, and General Electric. With the team members in place, Kevin took them all out to dinner, renting a private room at a restaurant near Amgen's headquarters in Thousand Oaks, a small town near Los Angeles. After a long meal that included shared laughs and ambitious plans for Amgen's future, Kevin shifted the tone, giving a brief speech at their first gathering that the team would remember for years to come. He hadn't planned what he was going to say, but after spending many years of his career navigating politics, he had clear ideas of what he was not going to put up with anymore. He said to the group:

Okay, sports fans, let's talk about how we're going to operate and some stuff that isn't going to work. The thing that for sure isn't going to work, besides all the obvious stuff like a lack of integrity, is politics. Politics means we don't tell each other the truth. Politics means you're disloyal; you've complained to somebody else, but you don't complain to us. Politics means you let your team work against somebody else's team, and maybe you don't actively direct it, but you tolerate it. Politics means you don't embody the values. Politics means you don't have a shared commitment to the mission. Politics means you trying to work me.

I've operated in environments where there were master politicians. I'm not a bad politician myself. How do you think I got this job? All this stuff is totally transparent to me. You know how when your four-year-old comes to you and they're transparent about how they're trying to work you? That's how you're going to look coming to me if you try any of this stuff. If any of you try to be politicians, I will know it, and I will fire you.

There was dead silence, but the talk had the desired effect. The guardrails of behavior were clear, and Kevin's leadership team stayed largely intact for the next decade.

. . .

In our work at Merryck & Co. with dozens of senior teams over the years, we typically start by asking the team members what they want from each other. In almost all cases, their response is the same: "We want to have each other's backs." It's shorthand for trust, of course—"I can count on you; we'll look out for each other; we'll support each other." We then ask them to share a team experience from when they were younger, and they will describe moments, perhaps from playing football or staging a theater production, when everyone pulled together, free of side agendas, to accomplish a big goal. They recognize that if they could just recapture that magic with their colleagues, it could be a powerful lift for them and their organization.

Yet this is often a big disconnect in business. As much as team members say they want to act like true teams, and to recapture a sense of camaraderie that they enjoyed outside their jobs, that level of trust and collaboration in the workplace is too often the exception rather than the rule. Yes, some level of dysfunction is to be expected, but it often can devolve into colleagues undermining each other. Some people engage in "pocket vetoes" by agreeing to a plan and not following through. Others are masters of micro-aggression, like smiling at odd moments in a meeting or building themselves up at a colleague's expense by saying, "I *actually* think that's a good idea." Some are always working the hallways before and after key meetings to advance their own agendas. These serial offenders set the tone for the team, and others are compelled to follow along or else suffer the consequences of being outmaneuvered. Each troubled team has its unique challenges. Tolstoy's famous line—"Happy families are all alike; every unhappy family is unhappy in its own way"—is just as true of leadership teams.

To shift the dynamic from dysfunction to function, and to pass the crucial test of building an effective team, leaders must wrestle with four questions that may appear simple but can be extraordinarily difficult: What is the purpose of the team? Who should be on the team? How will the team work together? What is the leader's role on the team? As we work through these questions, keep in mind that the lessons that we are drawing from CEOs and their leadership teams can be applied to teams at all levels.

What Is the Purpose of the Team?

When Satya Nadella took over as CEO of Microsoft in 2014, his direct reports were one of his chief areas of focus to begin the cultural turnaround that fueled record earnings and led the company to its trillion-dollar stock market valuation. "The thing I'm most focused on today is, how am I maximizing the effectiveness of the leadership team, and what am I doing to nurture it?" Nadella told Adam shortly after he moved into his new role. "A lot of people on the team were my peers, and I worked for some of them in the past. The framing for me is all about getting people to commit and engage in an authentic way, and for us to feel that energy as a team. I'm not evaluating them on what they say individually. None of them would be on this team if they didn't have some fantastic attributes. I'm only evaluating us collectively as a team. Are we able to authentically communicate, and are we able to build on each person's capabilities to the benefit of our organization?" He also addressed the foundational question of a team's purpose: "The framework we came up with is the notion that our purpose is to bring clarity, alignment, and intensity. What is it that we want to get done? Are we aligned in order to be able to get it done? And are we pursuing that with intensity? That's really the job."

Nadella was asking and answering questions that leaders sometimes overlook. What does success look like for the leadership team as a whole, rather than what are individual members of the team delivering on their own? The answer may seem self-evident. Leadership teams have always been a fixture of org charts to make sure there is alignment among different departments and divisions. But when leadership teams get together, the meetings often are structured around a series of updates to the CEO, with everyone stealing glances at their phones while they wait their turn to speak. If there is an agenda, it is largely filled with short-term tactical issues rather than longer-term strategic questions.

But to the question "Why are we a team in the first place?" there should only be one answer: to work together *on tasks and setting priorities that are best executed as a team.* What are the big strategic lifts that need the combined force of the entire team or subgroups of the team? Maybe internal cultural challenges need everyone's attention, or industry dynamics are demanding a faster timetable for a digital transformation. These are the sprawling "How are we going to do this?" questions that no individual member of the team can answer alone. Such joint projects have to be considered part of senior executives' responsibilities, in addition to running and advocating for their own teams. "I like to think of it as people needing to be dual citizens," said Helene Gayle, CEO of The Chicago Community Trust, a nonprofit. "You've got to be thinking about your own interests but also wearing that broader corporate hat."

If the team hopes to make progress on complex projects that require its combined muscle, then there can't be more than three or four priorities for any given quarter. If you have more than that, energy will be diffused. But prioritization is notoriously hard for teams, which can quickly draw up long lists of projects, some of them narrowly defined, that need to be tackled, said Harry Feuerstein, the former CEO of Siemens Government Technologies who now leads Merryck's leadership team practice. "When you look at the priorities of the average team, most of them don't fit within the scope of the team's collective responsibility and are often way outside the available bandwidth, so things don't get done," he added. He once asked a team to share with him its priorities, and there were 172 items on the list.

To be sure, adopting a "less is more" mindset also can be hard for ambitious executives, who often feel a sense of urgency to accomplish a lot quickly. "You simply can't do everything," said Lori Dickerson Fouché, the former CEO of TIAA Financial Solutions. "There were times I would walk into a new job, and my eyes would be huge and I would feel like a kid in a candy shop. I'd think, 'Let's just get after it,' instead of, 'OK, let's pause. What's the most important thing to really get after?' Being able to say 'no' or 'not now' were important lessons for me." This discipline ties back to the simple plan that we described in the first chapter, a key component of which is identifying the three or four big strategic levers you have to pull to accomplish the overarching goal of your organization.

Who Should Be on the Team?

In our mentoring work with senior leaders, we ask executives to tell us about the performance of their team members. Their answer often goes something like this: "They're great. Good people. Loyal. Hard-working." Then we like to point out that they are talking about general attributes, rather than answering the specific question we asked about performance—what are their objectives, and how well is each member performing against them? Then, after they talk about each team member in more depth, discussing their strengths and weaknesses, there is often a long pause, followed by a reluctant acknowledgment: "Maybe my team isn't as good as I thought they were."

Leaders' loyalty to their team members is understandable and laudable, up to a point. They bet on them when they hired them (and every leader would like to believe they are good judges of talent). The intensity of the job also forms powerful bonds, given that members of a leadership team spend more time with each other than with their families. They go through highs and lows together, and they get to know their colleagues at a deeply human level. Plus, the prospect of moving someone off the team creates its own risks for leaders. How will the rest of the group react? Will their replacement have their own set of challenges that emerge once the honeymoon is over?

That's how the slippery slope of tolerating substandard performance starts. Leaders invent narratives about why they can't act on their doubts, deciding that they need to make the most of the team they have, in much the same way that they put up with frustrating relatives. "The problem I generally see is that the CEO is hanging on to people too long or they don't have the right people in the right chairs," said Greg Brenneman of CCMP Capital. "People are very reluctant to change. The really good CEOs and management teams I've seen are not all that reluctant to morph themselves over time to do that. Even in really good companies, you'll find you only have 75 percent of the right people. In really bad ones, it's probably only 25 percent."

> ## "Even in really good companies, you'll find you only have 75 percent of the right people. In really bad ones, it's probably only 25 percent."
> **—Greg Brenneman, Executive Chairman, CCMP Capital**

Who should stay and who should go? Some calls are easy. The biggest worry about the stars on the team is how long they'll stick around before they get recruited to a bigger job, so make sure they're challenged and appreciated. You can't put up with the naysayers who always know why something is a bad idea or won't work. The "yay-sayers" who think everything the boss says is brilliant can't stick around either. Some people simply lack the intellectual horsepower for the job, or they are poisonous to the team dynamic. Then there are the passive-aggressive types who will say yes in a meeting but then not act on the plan. And if you don't get rid of these clear problem actors on the team, everyone else will respect you less as a leader. When you finally do, they will wonder what took you so long.

The trickiest calls about talent are the people who are on the bubble. They check many boxes, but as the leader, you have some concerns. What's the framework for making decisions about whether to keep them on the team? One way is to ask yourself this quick gut-check question: Who on your team would you rehire if all the positions on your team suddenly were open again? Or consider using the following leaders' approaches for gauging the strength of talent on a team:

Ron Williams, the former CEO of Aetna, assessed members of his team on the quality of their "forward radar," meaning their understanding of how they needed to evolve to help the company drive its growth strategy. "Is everyone on your team scaling at the pace they need to scale? Is everyone getting 15 percent better? People can start thinking, 'If I just keep doing what I'm doing, that's OK,'" Williams said. "But the world has become dramatically more challenging. Your business is bigger. It's more complex technologically. You've got to master those shifts. You are never done. What you see is that some people aren't evolving with the complexity of the business, and their 'forward radar' is diminished and keeps getting diminished."

David Politis, the CEO of BetterCloud, a software company, looks for three signs that somebody is not ready for the next growth stage:

One of the big tells is when I'm repeatedly seeing things in their part of the business that they're not seeing themselves. If I'm consistently the one to call out a fire happening in their part of the business that they were not aware of, that has always been one of the red flags for me. That's happened a number of times. It's also happened a number of times where people, because they weren't confident in their own abilities, didn't want to bring in a team that essentially could replace them. You always want to hire people who are better than you. But with some people, they worry about putting themselves and their own job at risk by bringing in strong people because they're not sure what they're doing. Another tell is when you're planning for the next year, and some people are asking to double the size of their team while someone else is asking to add just one more person. They can't visualize that next phase of growth, and of what's possible.

Bruce Gordon, the former CFO of the Disney Interactive Media Group, advises leaders to apply a "golden age" test to their teams:

It can be very difficult at times to make tough decisions about people who report to you. Very few people are bad at their job, but many are not as good as they must be. People have a hard time getting over that hump of saying, you're a really good person and you're really good technically, but you don't have the level of strategic and operational chops that I need. So it becomes a qualitative decision, not a quantitative decision. And that is a very difficult one for many people, including me when I was in senior positions. One benchmark is what I believe it means to have a golden age of management with your executive team. In my thirty years at Disney, I only had three golden ages, and they each lasted about two to three years.

After that, people get promoted. In a golden age, every single person on the team is not only aligned with the strategy, goals, values, and objectives, but they are also really good in their own right. And the best thing about golden ages is that they are so much fun. When you have that, the sum is much greater than the parts. And so the test becomes, "Will this person allow you to create a golden age?" Then you can have a conversation about the risks of replacing the person or not replacing the person.

"Very few people are bad at their job, but many are not as good as they must be."
—Bruce Gordon, former CFO, Disney Interactive Media Group

Setting the bar for performance doesn't have to rest entirely on the leader's shoulders. The team itself can work together to decide what good looks like by developing a shared set of criteria to evaluate the performance of every member on the team. Shortly after becoming CEO, Kevin initiated just such a project at Amgen, drawing inspiration from his time in the navy, where he read the *Engineering Department Organization and Regulations Manual*, written by Admiral Hyman G. Rickover. In that short book, Rickover, who led the development of nuclear-powered submarines, codified the behaviors he expected of every navy officer operating a nuclear vessel. At Amgen, Kevin brought together his leadership team for a four-hour off-site to start the process of writing its own guidelines. Drafts were then circulated among the top one hundred leaders at the company so that they could weigh in and feel a sense of shared ownership of the document.

After an exhaustive editing process, the group came up with the following leadership behaviors that would be expected of every Amgen senior executive:

Charts the course

- Translates the business strategy into challenging, actionable objectives and plans

- Conveys a sense of purpose and mission that motivates others

- Maintains direction, balancing big-picture concerns with day-to-day issues

- Develops insightful strategies based on deep knowledge of external and internal operating environments

Develops the best team

- Recruits and retains high-performing individuals and develops successors for key positions

- Builds diverse and empowered teams

- Provides honest and constructive feedback on an ongoing basis

Delivers results

- Consistently achieves results in line with Amgen values

- Establishes high performance standards, uses measurable goals to track progress, and continually raises the bar on performance and expectations

- Focuses their organization on high-impact activities by clearly communicating expectations, accountabilities, and responsibilities

- Conducts periodic reality-based results-focused operating reviews and drives quick corrective actions

---

> ## "Is everyone on your team scaling at the pace they need to scale?"
>
> **—Ron Williams, former Chairman and CEO, Aetna**

Role model

- Lives the Amgen values and sets expectations for others to do so

- Displays self-awareness and seeks self-improvement

- Demonstrates technical mastery of the job

- Champions opportunities for change and innovation

- Has the courage and judgment to take appropriate risks

Those criteria, which are still used at Amgen today with slight modifications, were used to guide an extended meeting every December in which the top fifteen leaders would gather to evaluate and discuss the one hundred executives below the C-suite level. And Kevin would also use the criteria to evaluate his direct reports. Because the expectations were clear to all, the focus of those conversations shifted from what Kevin thought of them to how they were performing against the criteria that they helped develop. "You can't just say, 'I'm going to make a gut call about somebody,'" Kevin says. "You've got to have objective criteria to assess the person to inform your judgment. You've got to know what good looks like."

As a leader, you are only going to be as good as the people on your team. Be clear in your mind what good looks like, and don't compromise. Nobody will thank you for keeping subpar players on your team, and you will be hurting your own chances of succeeding.

How Will the Team Work Together?

Paradoxically, some senior executives who lead teams aren't practiced at being part of a team. After all, they are so used to leading teams as they move up the ranks that they can be uncomfortable in a team setting where they have less control. Executives at all levels also tend to focus their energies on managing up (their boss) or down (their direct reports), rather than building relationships with their peers. Compensation for leadership teams can also reward silo behavior, with people's bonuses based on their individual P&Ls rather than the performance of the overall team. That's how the zero-sum mindset starts, with people thinking, "If I help you to improve your scoreboard, then that is going to hurt my scoreboard." The leader of the team must provide a counterweight to these forces.

"Corporations are a team sport."
—Dinesh Paliwal, former Chairman and CEO, Harman International

---

At Harman International, Dinesh Paliwal used pay structures to send a clear signal that collaboration matters. At the highest levels of the company, executives' bonuses were tied 100 percent to the overall performance of Harman. He knew that there were some detractors of this approach, given that the topic would come up during annual meetings of the company's top 150 leaders. "You learn during cocktail hours that there are some nonbelievers," Paliwal said. "Once people are a little comfortable, they will start to say, 'I busted my rear end and I see someone next to me benefiting from that.'" He would then remind them that there are inevitable ups and downs over the long term, and that perhaps three years earlier they benefited because one of their colleagues performed better than they did. "I'm not saying we're democratic, and that everybody should be compensated in the same way," Paliwal said. "I am saying that individuals don't win, and that corporations are a team sport."

Nobody should expect that assembling a group of high-achieving executives and calling them a team will make them act like a team. There are natural tensions built into different roles, and sorting out who has decision rights can be a fraught process. There will be elephants in the room, and they should be introduced and discussed to ensure the team is operating well together.

Consider the process that unfolded not long after John Donahoe took over as CEO of the cloud computing company ServiceNow in 2017. Six months after moving into his role, Donahoe held a leadership off-site with his team to sharpen their priorities and drive the next phase of growth for ServiceNow. As each executive talked about their goals, it became clear to everyone just how cross-functional those priorities were, and how much they were going to have to tighten up as a unit if they were going to succeed, particularly since three distinct groups made up the team—those who had been at the company for years, those who had joined shortly before Donahoe was appointed, and another third group that he had personally recruited. "It wasn't about being a team for team's sake," said Donahoe. "It was grounded in the idea that we can't get done what we want to get done unless we operate effectively as a team. In many ways, that is as much driven by the team as it is driven by the leader."

Donahoe had recruited Pat Wadors to be his chief talent officer, and she suggested to her colleagues that the team should develop its own "social contract," an exercise she had used when she was running HR at LinkedIn. At their off-site, the ServiceNow executives split into a few groups and set to work with flip charts, sticky notes, and markers. At one point, they surprised Donahoe by asking him to leave the room so the team could brainstorm by itself. He agreed, recognizing that there were some conversations that they needed to work through on their own. Once he rejoined them, they shared the bullet points they had drafted:

- We are a team first.

- We build trust and have each other's back.

- We work east-west.

- We don't tolerate ambiguity; we create and role-model decision clarity for ourselves and for our teams.

- We debate like we're right, listen like we're wrong, and then decide, commit, and lead together.

- We make each other better.

- We stay connected and celebrate each other's success.

- We keep our team healthy, supporting each other and striving for balance in our lives. We role-model one plus one plus one equals magic.

Some of the bullet points on that list were meant to set a tone, while others were intended to codify specific behaviors. "We work east-west" is a reminder to the team members to work through problems together first, to the degree they can, before escalating them "north" to Donahoe to solve. As a sign of its commitment to its social contract, the leadership team had it painted on the wall outside its offices in ServiceNow's headquarters in Santa Clara for all to see. "At the end of the day, teams have to feel like it's in their best interest to operate as a high-performance team, and that they can't win without that," said Donahoe, who later moved on to become CEO of Nike. "And the key to a high-performance team is having high-trust-based relationships, having a series of operating principles or a social contract, and then a commitment to each other to keep those up."

> "There's really only two kinds of days—ones when your team gets better and ones when your team gets worse."
> —Tobi Lütke, founder and CEO, Shopify

Building a true team dynamic, where people help each other, takes time and effort. In the crush of deadlines and packed schedules, spending time to really know each other and discuss the "how" of working together can seem like an unaffordable luxury. And while retreats with ropes courses or "trust falls" may help, the kind of social contract exercise that ServiceNow used will have far more impact, because it creates clear guardrails for behaviors, giving people license to call each other out if they fail to live up to their shared commitments to each other.

Though measuring how well a team works together isn't easily quantifiable, Tobi Lütke, the CEO of Shopify, an e-commerce platform, adopted an intriguing metric after he shifted from his role as an individual contributor to being responsible for the team's success:

> The hardest thing for me was to rewrite my own value system to be compatible with my new role. I felt really good about being a computer programmer. It took me years to realize that a day where I met with investors and spoke at a conference was actually not a wasted day. Intellectually I knew this, but internally it just didn't feel like it. I had to systematically rebuild how I measured my own contribution. Once I did that, I started realizing that it's the team that matters, and that the best way for me to spend any given day is to essentially figure out how to make my team a tiny bit better. Because there's really only two kinds of days—ones when your team gets better and ones when your team gets worse. And if you just spend time getting better, then over a prolonged period of time you become essentially unbeatable.

What Is the Leader's Role on the Team?

Surprising as this may seem, many leaders are not that concerned with building a healthy team dynamic. Some prefer more of a hub-and-spoke system, where they see the whole picture and meet with direct reports individually rather than as a group. Or they take more of a hands-off approach and then scratch their heads in frustration when their team doesn't get along. Or they believe that people operate at their best when they feel insecure and anxious, so the leader encourages discord in the name of "creative tension" by playing people off each other, so that colleagues spend more time watching their backs than having each other's backs.

But make no mistake, the leader must accept full responsibility for ensuring that the team is successful. Yes, a leader's job description can seem endless at times, but a big part of the role is ensuring that the team is working well together, coaching everyone to continually improve and grooming a successor. Here are some of the key responsibilities that come up time and again across conversations with hundreds of CEOs.

Psychological Safety

The team leader creates an environment of psychological safety, so that people are comfortable being open and candid with each other. "Like a lot of people, I've worked in companies before with what I call a 'stump a chump' culture," said Kathy Savitt, a former CEO who's held leadership roles at companies that include Yahoo and Amazon. "That's when a CEO or a leader will throw out a question and somebody will offer an answer. But nobody else has the courage to answer, and yet everyone then critiques the answer that the one person offered. Or you do something creatively and then everyone else in the company calls out what they would change, yet they haven't put either the professional or the personal passion behind actually creating something of value. I've been on management teams that have done that, and it's very toxic."

Clear Agendas

The team leader sets clear agendas for meetings. "It's not about being the decider; it's about facilitating the steps to get to the right decision," said Marcus Ryu of Guidewire. "It really is the superpower of the CEO to exercise to say, 'I want half an hour on this topic and I want these people here, and at the end I want a decision on whether we're going east or west, and we're not leaving until that's decided.'"

Clear Rules of Debate

The team leader clarifies the rules of debate and decision making. "One of the things we do is try to be very clear about decisions, because there's this built-in tension between hearing people's opinions and people thinking everything's a democracy," said Carl Bass, the former CEO of Autodesk, a design software company. "We're very clear at the beginning of every meeting whether it's one person's decision, or whether it's more of a discussion to reach consensus. It's a really valuable thing to understand because otherwise people can feel frustrated that they gave out their opinions, but they don't understand the broader context for the final decision. One of the main roles for a leader is to get as many opinions as possible on the table. But the flip side of that is you have to be clear when you're asking people for information and opinion but not turning over the ability to make the decision to them."

Inclusive Conversations

The team leader draws everyone into the conversation and, if the stakes are high, ensures that everyone has a chance to speak. "One of the things I would do in important team meetings," says Kevin, "is to go around the table and say, 'What do you think? What do you think? And what about you?' I wouldn't always go around the table in the same order and I wouldn't always start with the same person. People understood I really wanted to know what they thought, and if it was clear we weren't aligned on an important topic, we'd talk some more."

Coaching

The team leader takes responsibility for coaching everyone on the team. Each December, over the holiday break, Kevin would write each of his direct reports a two-page letter that would cover three points—what the executive did well that year and how much Kevin appreciated their efforts and why; what he was counting on them to do in the coming year; and the three things that the executive should focus on to raise their game as a leader. He would meet with them in person to discuss the letter once everyone was back at work in January, and again halfway through the year to discuss progress. "After those forty-five-minute meetings, I wanted them to have complete confidence and clarity that they understood what I thought about their performance and what I expected of them," he adds. "Those letters came to be seen by the people as the single-most important communication they had about their development."

Talent Scout

The team leader owns the role of talent scout. Teams are not static, nor should they be. People come and go, and sometimes they need to be replaced with an executive who can help carry the company through the next phase of growth. That may mean going outside the organization, and the leader can't rely just on others, including executive recruiters, to find the best candidate. Kevin regularly asked his business acquaintances outside of Amgen for the names of the most talented executives they knew in certain positions. Those executives may not have been willing to leave their current jobs at the time, but if they were passed over for a key promotion, or if their company were acquired, they suddenly could be more open to considering an offer. In both cases, that's how Kevin found his head of R&D and head of sales and marketing when he was building his leadership team. "You can't just say to yourself that I'm going to start looking for talent," Kevin says. "You have to be on the lookout for talent all the time."

Grooming a Successor

Team leaders groom their successor. This is not a natural impulse for many leaders, who for various reasons would prefer to put off thinking about who might take over for them when they move on. But spotting and grooming a successor is part of the talent scout and coach role of the leader. For example, Kevin was on the lookout early on for somebody who might be able to take over for him someday. Five years into his twelve-year tenure as CEO, he met Bob Bradway, who at the time headed investment banking in Europe for

Morgan Stanley. He checked all the right leadership boxes, and Kevin convinced Bradway, who was open to a new challenge, to take a pay cut and join the ranks of a hundred other executives at the VP level at Amgen. After Bradway succeeded in every new job he was given, he was elevated to president, and Kevin mentored him for two years before passing the baton to him in 2012. Since then, Amgen's stock has risen from roughly $70 a share to more than $200 a share, and in 2020 Amgen's stock was added to the Dow Jones Industrial Average, an acknowledgment of the company's long-term success and growth. "Your legacy is ultimately determined by two simple tests," says Kevin. "Is the enterprise better on the day you left than when you took over? And how does your successor perform?"

"The top three keys to success are the team you build, the team you build, and the team you build."

— Shellye Archambeau, former CEO, MetricStream

. . .

Building, managing, and developing a team can seem like a full-time job on its own, but the investment of time will pay significant dividends for leaders if they answer these foundational questions to ensure that the team is operating at its highest possible level: What is our purpose? Do we have the best people on the team? Are we clear on how we're going to work together? Am I, as the leader, owning the responsibilities of running the team and personally coaching everyone to get better? Many leaders fail this threshold test, and they won't remain in their jobs for long without a strong team to execute the strategy. And while many leaders understand the importance of teams intellectually, they don't always act on it because they allow people on their teams to put their personal agendas first, because they have trouble recruiting people, because they can't make people work together well, because they lack the courage to coach people to improve, and because they shrink from tough decisions to remove subpar players. If you don't surround yourself with great people, you will find yourself doing their jobs instead of doing your job. Across interviews with hundreds of leaders, the theme is reinforced time and again: There is simply no substitute for a great team.

"The top three keys to success are the team you build, the team you build, and the team you build," said Shellye Archambeau, the former CEO of MetricStream, a provider of governance, risk and compliance software. "And I mean build in an active sense, because as the company grows and develops and evolves, the same needs to be true for the team. That can be hard, because you work closely with these people, but you have to bring the team forward. It's about always thinking about the team that you need three years from now."

Test #4
Can You Lead Transformation?

The status quo is enormously powerful, and it is the enemy of change.

G iven that transformation is now a fixture of every leader's job description, and since there is no more dangerous position in business than muddling along and clinging to the status quo, perhaps it's time for the phrase "leading change" to be declared redundant. To lead is to change and it requires refining how your company operates today while simultaneously disrupting yourself before someone else does.

Yes, it can be difficult enough to master the challenges we've described in the previous three chapters—to crystallize a simple plan, build a high-performing team, and create a culture that aligns everyone on behaviors that drive the strategy. The challenge of remaking and reinventing almost every aspect of a company on an ongoing basis can be overwhelming for many leaders, particularly because employees tend to prefer sameness over uncertainty, especially the uncertainty caused by disruption (nothing can set a company on edge faster than a CEO who starts asking a lot of what-if questions). Faced with the prospect of trying to overcome the powerful inertia of the status quo, some leaders instead kick the can down the road, telling themselves that their successor can deal with all the disruptive forces after they have stepped down. Or perhaps they hire a chief digital officer to handle the transformation, not recognizing that the person is likely to be pushed to the sidelines by colleagues who want to protect their empires.

What are the keys to driving transformation? Our approach here is not to provide you with an eight-step process. Such frameworks are readily available elsewhere, and their usefulness can be limited by the simple fact that no single playbook can address the unique challenges that each company faces. Our focus instead is to discuss transformation through the lens of leadership and draw lessons from case studies that will be useful for any executive who is embarking on an effort to drive change. The examples that we share—the New York Times Company, Amgen, and BetterCloud—represent companies in a range of sizes and industries. Most important, though, they reflect different degrees of the urgency with which they had to address the need to transform themselves. For example, Amgen had just come through a long period of rapid growth under Kevin's leadership and needed to overhaul and streamline its operations for its next phase of growth. The New York Times Company, contending with a precipitous drop in print advertising, had a more urgent challenge to shift its business model to be able to sustain itself as a digital company. And BetterCloud, confronted with an existential threat because of rapid changes in cloud computing, had to "burn the boats" and build a new platform from scratch.

The themes that emerge from the experiences of these three companies help illustrate the key approaches that every leader should keep in mind as they embark on their own transformation efforts. They include:

- Enlist allies to build an unassailable case for the need to change so that everyone understands why the status quo is not an option.

- Clarify what is not going to change, particularly mission and purpose, to make employees more open to new approaches for accomplishing their work.

- Engage your team and others throughout the organization to develop the transformation strategies so that there is a sense of shared ownership (top-down plans don't work).

- Be transparent and communicate relentlessly at all stages of the process.

- Ensure commitment is shared by the CEO and the top leadership team to implement the plan with clear lines of responsibilities and a scoreboard to measure progress and success.

- Acknowledge the uncertainty but reinforce the certainty of the need to change and the confidence that the organization can be nimble to adjust.

As we share their stories, you'll no doubt spot other insights that are applicable to your own organization. Again, every company's challenges are unique, but there are approaches that have universal applicability across every effort.

The New York Times Company

When a headhunter first contacted Mark Thompson about whether he would want to be considered for the CEO job at the New York Times, he said no. Friends also advised Thompson, a veteran BBC executive, to steer clear, in part because the hidebound traditions of the Times would make change nearly impossible. Ultimately, though, he made the leap, particularly after he became convinced that the Ochs-Sulzberger family that controlled the paper, along with the Times's board of directors, were committed to shaking things up. "I concluded that if the organization would get out of its own way, it could do three or four times better," he said.

He joined when there were big question marks about how the Times would survive the steep and steady drop in revenue from print advertising that had been the financial lifeblood of the company for decades. The company had to grow its digital operation but the print paper, a mature business, still remained the primary focus of the newsroom. And because of the traditional wall between the news and business sides that exists to protect the journalists' independence, many in the newsroom were disinclined to engage in discussions to help their business colleagues find answers to the financial challenges.

For Thompson, his guiding principle as he took over the role was not to assume that he had the answer, or that he was expected to come up with one. "You are not going to succeed as a CEO if you try to impose a set of ideas or a new culture on Day 1," he said. "It just doesn't work. It's got to be owned. It's more a question of trying to pull it out of the organization rather than to push it in, and that meant trying step-by-step to encourage a deeper conversation about the future."

Because of that historical divide between the newsroom and the business side, he knew that the journalists would view any plans that he championed with some skepticism. So he turned the tables and encouraged the newsroom to pull together a group to study big questions of how the news side could become more innovative. That committee was led by A. G. Sulzberger, who at the time was an editor in the newsroom and is now the publisher of the paper (Adam, one of the authors of this book, was recruited by Sulzberger to be part of that innovation committee). The group took more than nine months to report and write its ninety-seven-page document, which was intended only for a small audience of senior leaders at the Times. But the report was leaked to BuzzFeed, which shared it with the world on May 15, 2014. Its blunt language about all the challenges inside the Times—"We have to look hard at our traditions and push ourselves," for example—was a deep-breath moment for an institution that prided itself on being considered the gold standard of journalism.

For all the initial worries about the report becoming public, however, it created that crucial shared understanding of the challenges the company faced, which is the necessary first step of any transformation effort. "The first day was brutal," recalled Sulzberger. "The headlines on the internet were about a devastating report, a scathing report, and the Times in chaos. I had no idea how my colleagues were going to take it. Like so many people in an institution that really cherishes its traditions, I probably was a cautious incrementalist in how I felt that change should be talked about. But after a day or two, it became really clear that the whole conversation was shifting—that the report felt scary to people but also profoundly empowering, and that for the first time they felt like they really understood the context in which their lives and days and work habits were all changing."

A key lesson for any company attempting its own state of the union report is that it should include only unassailable facts. Sulzberger said:

> I wanted the final innovation report to consist entirely of stuff that was unequivocally true. It's so easy, if you have a big document and platform to articulate your view of the future, to throw a lot of your pet ideas in there. Someone might say, "I think the way we write stories should change like this," or "We should be looking for these particular qualities in leaders." But that model is problematic for getting a consensus around the need to change, because you're introducing ideas that reasonable people can disagree with. And once you've introduced ideas that reasonable people can disagree with, you've created a relationship with your recommendations that feels like it could be a matter of opinion. What I wanted was to fly at an

altitude where we were certain about every recommendation that we included. Our statements were backed by data, and even with the things that were softer, they were things that you plainly couldn't argue with.

Once the report became public, Sulzberger embarked on an internal road show, meeting for ninety minutes with groups that were capped at roughly thirty people. In all, he met with about twelve hundred journalists. He learned through those conversations the importance of communicating the "why" behind all the new demands on journalists, including building a presence on social media, filing stories faster, and making articles more visual. Sulzberger said:

> We never really laid out the framework. So you had this profound dissonance of an executive team really versed in the challenges and why we needed to change, and then you had most of the company, the people who actually do the great work that makes this place special, just being told that they had to change without explaining the broader dynamics. In journalism, we have this saying, "Show, don't tell." And we had never shown the problem. We had never given our colleagues the chance to own the problem with us and own the challenge with us. We were just telling them that we had to change. Another big takeaway, and a surprise, was just how much appetite there was in the newsroom for conversations about the report. Many people said they couldn't remember the last time they had been a part of an open, searching conversation about

the company, our strategy, and how we're executing. It's just a reminder that communication is often the last item on the checklist but it's always the most important.

To help allay many of the fears and concerns about whether the Times would be straying from its roots, Sulzberger invoked an expression he had heard from Dean Baquet, the executive editor: for an institution to change, it needs to separate mission from tradition. "Mission should never be tinkered with," Sulzberger explained. "You mess with mission at your own risk. Tradition needs to be constantly interrogated. Now tradition isn't necessarily bad. There are traditions that, once you interrogate them, hold up perfectly. And some companies undergoing change will tear up tradition for the sake of tearing up tradition, and that's a mistake. But traditions also shouldn't be kept around for their own sake."

"You mess with mission at your own risk. Tradition needs to be constantly interrogated."

—A. G. Sulzberger, publisher, *New York Times*

To do that effectively, leaders need to be crystal clear about their company's reason for being. Sulzberger said:

If everything is up for grabs, if you can change literally anything about a company, then the company has no reason for being. And if the company has no reason for being, then some younger, hungrier startup should come and displace you anyway. Once you're able to articulate your reason for being and what's not going to change, that needs to be communicated really aggressively throughout the company. And if your answer to that is persuasive, it gives people more permission to lean into change. For us, our journalism was not going to change, but everything else can change if it will better service that mission. A big part of my job in terms of communicating with the newsroom staff was getting everyone to understand that we were all aligned around that, which gave everyone permission to sign on for the journey.

Any leader making the case for necessary transformation is going to encounter skepticism from employees. Will the new plan work? The uncertainty has to be acknowledged and addressed head-on. Sulzberger said:

Inevitably, if you are leading change in an organization, you're going to try some things that will work and some things that won't work. And when some of the things don't work, you're going to stop doing them, and some people are going to say, "See, you guys don't really know what you're doing. You're wasting our time. A year ago, you said that this was going to be a big thing and today it's just disappeared altogether." One of the ways I've dealt with that is to say, "There is no playbook for us. We are not following a map here. We are blazing a trail. And we are going to try some things that will work, and we will try some things that won't work, and it may be a waste of your time. And a year from now you may be grumbling at me and saying, why did you ever think this was a good idea at all? But here's why we're trying it and here's what we hope it will do for us if it does work. And if it doesn't, I'll explain why."

The innovation report helped create momentum for change, but the company overall still needed a unifying strategy for leading through its transformation. The old model, which relied heavily on revenue from advertisers, was under threat, as more advertisers were moving their dollars to Facebook and Google. Subscriptions to the print paper had also been a reliable source of revenue in the past, but with more readers getting the news on their phones and computers, the company had to build a new business model for a digital future.

In 2015, CEO Mark Thompson started a regular meeting of what came to be known as the "Friday Group," involving the top leaders from the business side and the newsroom. For six months, they met each Friday, starting at noon and finishing at around 6 p.m. Thompson knew that the group would have to persevere through some tough discussions to land together on some new insights. "Until we could have a genuinely productive and honest conversation at the top, we weren't going to get anywhere," Thompson recalled. "And I was happy to wait. You have to be quite patient. I've seen people come into media organizations and try to get dramatic shifts quickly. They tend to be rejected by the antibodies. Many people in the Friday

Group were skeptical at first and simply wanted to get back to their busy jobs. We started off talking about the challenges, and by the summer, the meetings were becoming difficult and fraught."

"I've seen people come into media organizations and try to get dramatic shifts quickly. They tend to be rejected by the antibodies."

—Mark Thompson, former President and

CEO, New York Times Company

One idea that emerged in those meetings provided a way to align the two halves of the company around a shared goal, captured in the phrase "subscription first." The idea was that a singular focus on attracting more digital subscribers would be good for both journalists (who would have more readers) and the business executives (more subscribers would be a reliable revenue source and also attract more advertising dollars). Eventually, and after some intense debate, the "subscriber first" strategy won over the group, and it has provided an important shared scoreboard for the entire company to track its growth. When Thompson was appointed CEO in 2012, it had just over 600,000 digital subscribers. In 2020, it passed the 5 million subscriber mark. And during his tenure, the stock price has more than quadrupled. In 2020, he passed the CEO baton to Meredith Kopit

Levien, whom he recruited in 2013 from Forbes to be chief revenue officer.

Amgen

During the two-decade stretch when Kevin served as president and then CEO of Amgen, the company's primary focus was growth. When his successor, Bob Bradway, took over, the new leadership team recognized that work was needed to get Amgen ready for the next phase of growth. The shorthand they used was that Amgen was "in a good spot, but . . ."

The "but" was that Amgen was like a thirty-five-year-old house with the original plumbing, windows, roof, and electrical systems. The infrastructure needed an upgrade. Some of Amgen's drugs were coming off patent (meaning big drops in revenue), new product launches needed funding, and the company was planning an expansion into dozens of additional countries. Amgen recognized that if it didn't make the necessary changes, someone was going to come along, whether a competitor or activist investors, and potentially force those changes from the outside. "We knew we were going to need several quarters to sell the idea internally and to get people moving, and a few quarters to make the changes," said Bradway. "So we knew that we had time, but not an abundance of it. It was really a case of changing before we have to."

Pressing for change is always harder when things are going well, but Amgen provides a useful case study on how to disrupt the status quo even when the need isn't evident to all. Amgen's leaders started with a simple mantra to start the necessary conversations around transformation: "Build a better company." "We wanted to create a language and a skill set and a methodology that would enable Amgen to keep changing a decade later," said Brian McNamee, chief human resources officer on Kevin's leadership team who was named chief transformation officer by Bradway. "Transformations can be serial events, but if done right, they turn into long-term continuous improvement capabilities," McNamee added. "So, the goal was to build that capability, to build a better company. We were very careful not to put anything underneath that at the outset, in terms of specifics."

Bradway and McNamee put a simple question on the table for the leadership team—How do we build a better company? But they did add some ground rules for the coming brainstorming sessions. For example, everybody was told they had to "concede to the middle," shorthand for signaling that members of the leadership team had to let go of any impulses to protect their respective parts of the business, and that the company's best interests were going to come first. That meant wrestling with some tough issues, like cost structures that needed to be reined in. "My role was to make sure they were brought into the discussion," McNamee said. "You've got to set the tone up front that these things are going to get put on the table; no more just talking about them in the hallway."

Bradway then recruited a team of high-potential younger executives inside Amgen, calling them the "Gang of 30," to explore new approaches to solving some of the company's challenges. But he also solicited ideas from all levels of the company, sending a clear signal that he wanted to hear every idea they had, even if they seemed a bit off the wall. And as chief transformation officer, one of McNamee's responsibilities was to ensure that members of the leadership team did not screen out any ideas. Bradway said:

> The organization needs to get comfortable with the notion that they can give us the full range of options and leave us to choose the sensible options. We were trying to give the organization confidence that people didn't have to eliminate the extreme options because they might be afraid that these idiots at the top will choose things that are harmful to the company. Very often, leaders on the rungs below will say, "I don't want to give them that option because I'm afraid they might choose it," or they'll think, "I'm stupid for putting it on the table." So we had to continuously give them confidence by saying that we want all the options. You have to just keep role-modeling that idea and keep insisting that they bring you the full range of options, even the things that they think are too extreme. Because then we can see that there are a lot of different ways to attack this.

For example, Amgen's development process for new drugs had long been split into two divisions—R&D and operations—which had created inefficiencies and silo behavior in the company. The team working on that initiative suggested that the two be combined so that programs could move faster, with fewer handoffs, and eliminate overlaps and redundancies. The leaders running the separate divisions, not surprisingly, resisted the notion, but once it was put on the table for the entire C-suite team to review, they made the decision to put them together. "This was a major change from the past, and sent a signal to the organization that this transformation was going to be different in that nothing was off the table in terms of options when it came to building the best company," McNamee said.

Bradway and McNamee also knew that the process of soliciting and sorting through ideas would have to be coupled with a deliberate communication plan to slowly win over the top five hundred people at the company about the need for the transformation. In business, after all, there is a widely used metaphor of the "frozen middle" of companies, referring to the layer of managers who, to preserve the status quo, keeping ideas from bubbling up from below and freezing out directives from above. But that frozen layer can be much higher in organizations than the leaders might want to believe. So Bradway and McNamee embraced the idea of creating a "sponsorship spine" to ensure that the level of leaders below the C-suite would themselves be won over about the need to change, so that they would champion the plan to their direct reports, who in turn would advocate for the need to change with their teams.

"The CEO can stand up and talk all he or she wants about making change, but at the end of the day, the manager in France or the team leader in Tampa, Florida, is going to go to a conference room and see what his or her direct boss thinks," Bradway said. "If his or her direct boss says, 'Yeah, we'll do the bare minimum,' or 'I don't know what it means, we'll figure it out later,' then there's no energy. If, on the other hand, you go into the conference room and your direct boss is saying, 'Here's what we're going to do,' and they're articulating the message in their own authentic voice rather than reading the CEO's script, that's the magic and that's what we did. We recognized that we needed to enlist five hundred people in the storytelling."

The transformation effort succeeded. It led to cost savings of $1.9 billion, faster growth, and bigger profit margins even as the company expanded into additional countries. After stepping down from Amgen in 2019, McNamee started consulting with other companies on their transformation efforts. One of the most common problems he sees is a false consensus among the leadership team members about the need for transformation in the first place. "One CEO I was working with told me, 'This is where we're going, and everybody agrees,'" McNamee said. "I told him, 'Give me an hour with six of your direct reports.' After I met with them I told the CEO, 'There's no agreement on the current state and there are wildly different views on how we got here.'"

> ## "I told the CEO, 'There's no agreement on the current state and there are wildly different views on how we got here.'"
> **—Brian McNamee, former Chief Transformation Officer, Amgen**

His experience is a powerful reminder that there has to be a shared understanding about the current state of affairs before meaningful discussions can start on what needs to change. "You have to stop and focus and make sure that you're building an objective view of what the current state is and not bending to the political sensitivities in the room," McNamee added. "It's like building a case for the need to change."

Given the success of the transformation at Amgen, other CEOs often reach out to Bradway for his advice. "I always start with the same question: Are you going to lead it or are you going to delegate it?" he said. "If CEOs delegate transformation, your organization figures it out overnight, and they will be less motivated to follow through. If the CEO is really on it and devoting energy to it, the organization figures that out as well. They realize, oh, I guess we really have to do this."

BetterCloud

Amgen and the New York Times were able to plan and execute their transformations from broad and solid foundations. They had clear missions and reasons for being, and they needed to reframe how they operate to build on their already well-established strengths.

But what are the lessons of transformation for the thousands of entrepreneurs who grind every day for new customers and for every additional dollar of revenue to build their companies and keep their investors off their backs? Yes, they must master the art of the pivot—the constant fine-tuning adjustments to better meet the demands of the customer. But what if your entire business model suddenly comes into question? Such existential threats require wholesale transformation, magnifying the challenges and accelerating the timetables for change in ways that provide powerful lessons for founders and their leadership teams.

Many CEOs of young companies are reluctant to share such stories, preferring to put up a confident front for their customers and investors. But David Politis of BetterCloud believes that startup CEOs should share the dark moments they face so that they can all learn from each other. "I think it's important as an entrepreneur to be open about the challenges, and not trying to live the Instagram life of only the really, really good things," he said. "If you ask entrepreneurs how they're doing, they almost always say, 'I'm killing it.' And you want to say that, but I couldn't hide what was happening at our company."

> "I think it's important as an entrepreneur to be open about the challenges, and not trying to live the Instagram life of only the really, really good things."
> —David Politis, founder and CEO, BetterCloud

Politis founded BetterCloud in 2011 on the idea that businesses were moving to the cloud by outsourcing their corporate data centers and needed more management and security for cloud applications. The company focused on only one specific application, Google Apps, now called G Suite. By 2015, the company had grown to about sixty employees and a thousand customers, but the technological land-scape was changing rapidly. It was as if it had constructed an office building with one kind of electrical outlet, and then suddenly all its tenants were demanding that the building be able to accommodate all the different plugs that are used worldwide. A software patch was not going to fix the problem; the company had to, in effect, open up the walls and completely redo the wiring. "All of a sudden our customers were saying about our core product, 'It's nice, but you're only handling this one small area,'" Politis recalled. "We realized we probably had a ceiling on our business, and that we were going to have to make some big shifts."

He pulled his top technology team into a meeting and presented the challenge to them. After a wide-eyed reaction to the implications of the problem, they said in disbelief: "We're going to have to rebuild from scratch." Because Politis wasn't a technologist by background, he was relying completely on his team of engineers to find the answer. "Having a team around you that's in the boat with you, and you trust them and can lean on them, is so important," he said. He formed a "tiger team" of his top technology and product leaders and announced the new direction to the entire staff in September 2015: "This is going to be a new chapter for the company."

One certainty for Politis was that he was going to be open with the entire company about the challenges that BetterCloud faced. It's an approach that he learned from an earlier CEO role. "At that smaller company, I essentially thought I shouldn't tell anybody anything, because if they know that anything was wrong, they're going to quit," he said. "Then 2008 came and we got hit with the financial crisis like everyone else, and we had to let go of half the company in a day. Everyone was surprised. We thought we were making all this money, they said. Clearly, I had not told them anything. I was so stressed. Someone gave me the advice, 'You can't have all of it on your shoulders. If you're the only person who knows about it, how can anyone else help to actually improve this or fix the situation?' I'll never forget that. Since then, I have always believed in transparency, good or bad."

While many of the employees were excited by the challenge, others were skeptical that the plan to rebuild the company from scratch was going to be possible. For Politis and his leadership team, it was a clarifying moment to realize who was willing to sign up for what turned out to be a two-year challenge, with no certainty that the plan would work. "One lesson from that time is that different stages of a company attract different risk profiles and different kinds of people, and the persona of the company started to change," he said. "The only people who were willing to stay on were people who wanted that challenge and that risk. We turned over a lot of people, and the people who stayed were the ones who were ready for the risks."

To keep people feeling as if they were making progress, even if the ultimate goal seemed far off, he adopted a strategy of celebrating small wins. "There were four pillars of the new technology, and every time we stood one of them up, we would send an email to the whole company to celebrate the milestone and explain why it was really important," he said. "As we were showing customers what we were doing, we would send their feedback to everyone. If we didn't tell people what was happening, people would have assumed the product's never coming out. The salespeople don't see the code being written. Even the engineers generally only see the code that they write. You have to constantly be telling people what's happening."

Despite the small wins, the board of directors of BetterCloud grew impatient a year into the transformation effort, as the timeline stretched beyond the initial deadlines. Politis recalled:

> They said, "What's going on? This is taking longer than ex-
> pected and we need to see something." The next day, we called
> an emergency all-hands meeting, which I had never done be-
> fore. I told everyone that the board meeting was like getting
> a root canal, and they were right to ask the questions they
> asked. This is not a research project. This is a business. We told
> everyone that we have to cut out anything that is not targeted
> at getting this platform out or selling the existing platform
> so that we continue to grow revenue. "If it's not one of those
> two things, stop working on that project immediately," I said.
> "Don't ask anyone. I'm not doing anything else. Neither should
> you, and that's it. If you don't want to be here, we're not going
> to be offended. We are in the grind now."

Throughout the process, Politis and his leadership team did hear concerns from employees who felt the company was changing directions too frequently. He addressed the concerns head-on at the next scheduled all-hands meeting. "I talked to them about Amazon and Google and some of the best technology companies in the world," he said. "Amazon started selling books and look at what their business is today. They didn't do that by just being bullheaded, putting their head down and running into a brick wall over and over. They went around it. I said that we're just trying to do the same thing. We don't know where we're going to end up. We may not be an Amazon or Google, but why, just for the sake of staying consistent in our strategy, should we look at a brick wall and run right into it?"

Getting the technology right solved just half of the problem. BetterCloud then had to convince customers to adopt it. Politis established a simple goal in January 2017 to rally everyone around: to sign up a hundred customers for the new platform over the next nine months. Yes, they had some relationships already in place that could get them in the door, but they were selling a new solution to a much more complicated problem. They knew they couldn't count on any easy wins. Politis said:

> It was a trying time, but the whole company had one goal.
> Literally every TV in both offices had a counter from zero to
> a hundred. That was the only thing that was on the TVs. We
> started at the beginning of 2017, and by the end of January
> we had one. In February, we added three more. In March,
> we had another six, and it was roughly the same for April. It
> was slow, and we had people asking, "How are we going to
> get to a hundred?" And by the way, we had no idea if we'd
> get to a hundred. That was the number that felt to me like
> critical mass. But we were all swimming together in one
> direction. The engineering team would say, "What do we
> need to do to get that customer on board?" Then we had

fifteen, and all of a sudden, the momentum started to build. We ultimately blew through our goal and ended September at around 140. We had a massive celebration, with champagne and balloons that said "100" on them. I will never forget those nine months. To limp along at first and then just crush the number at the end was incredible. People were crying. It was crazy.

The transformation has continued to pay dividends, and the company has grown quickly by every measure. Average revenue per account is ten times higher than it was in 2015. The average length of its contracts has stretched from one year to two-and-a-half years. The company's revenues grew from about $10 million in 2015 to more than $65 million.

> "To limp along at first and then just crush the number at the end was incredible. People were crying. It was crazy."
> —David Politis, founder and CEO, BetterCloud

Another lasting impact from the effort is that Politis, when he is talking to job candidates and potential new investors, tries to scare them off by talking about the challenges the company faces in the coming years, rather than selling them on the best-case scenario.

"Instead of overselling where the company stands, it's better to share the good, the bad, and the ugly, so that you know someone's going to be in the boat with you when problems come up," he said. "The best people, the ones who are still on the team now, are the ones that say to you after you lay out all the problems in the interview, 'That's solvable. It's going to take me some time, but I want to attack that.'"

. . .

Making the case for change can be easier for companies like Better-Cloud and the Times, which faced clear and present dangers, with trend lines on revenue and profits that were plainly unsustainable and that removed the status quo as an option. If there is an iceberg dead ahead, it will be harder for people to say that they should stay the course. For companies where the threats are more amorphous and less immediate, like Amgen's in 2012, the challenge is exponentially harder. Why fix it if it isn't broken? Resistance to change is strong enough even when the need is urgent, but it can seem impossible when everything appears fine on the surface. Even though the very best time to change is when things are going well, the leadership challenge always is going to be harder when there are no obvious reasons to take urgent action.

Regardless of the particular circumstances of your organization, the themes we highlighted at the outset, and illustrated through the stories of the Times, Amgen, and BetterCloud are relevant and useful for all leaders. These are the foundations of a leadership playbook for transformation:

- Enlist allies to build the case for change.

- Be clear about what is not going to change as you engage the organization to help develop the new strategies.

- Be transparent and communicate relentlessly.

- Ensure commitment is shared by top leaders to implement the plan, with clear lines of responsibilities and a scoreboard to measure progress.

- Acknowledge the uncertainty while balancing it with the confidence in the team, the new direction, and the ability to adjust on the fly.

Transformation is not a onetime event. It is an ongoing challenge that requires leaders to balance refining how the company operates today while also recognizing the need for constant disruption. It is, in many ways, a mindset to be able to question everything you're doing even as you're making decisions about short- and long-term strategies. That may sound like a recipe for paralysis, but it is also a worthwhile goal to which every leader should aspire—to keep reinventing themselves so that they can reinvent their companies. There can be no status quo, for the leaders themselves or the businesses they are leading.

Bracken Darrell, the CEO of Logitech, said:

> As you go forward, the more successful you are, the more
> you have to break things or create this sense of urgency, be-
> cause people tend to not want to change things when they're

working. So, I am much more focused on changing things on a regular basis now, much more ambiguous than probably the people who work for me like, and much more intuitive about what I really dig into. I'm very explicit about it. I've shared a story from 2018, after I'd been on the job for five years. One Sunday night, I asked myself, "Am I the right person for the next five years?" I had made tons of change, and the stock was up about 500 percent. I knew that, on paper, I probably was the right person for the next five years, and that it's risky to change if you don't have to. On the other hand, I had been involved in every single personnel and strategic decision. My disadvantage was that I knew too much, and that I was too embedded in everything we were doing . . .

"I decided that I was going to fire myself, and that I would sleep on the decision."

—Bracken Darrell, President and CEO, Logitech

So I decided that I was going to fire myself, and that I would sleep on the decision. I didn't share it with anybody, including my wife or kids. I just thought to myself that I might be done. I woke up the next morning and felt that I knew exactly what I needed to do: I have to rehire myself but have no sacred cows. It was super exciting and fun, and I started changing things that I had put in place. Fortunately, I didn't have to change things radically, but I felt new again. Then I realized that the real opportunity is to compress that time frame from five years to a year and then to a month and then into every day. And if you can get yourself to the point where you can really come in unbiased every day, then you're there. That's my ultimate goal, which I think is impossible, but that's the goal.

Test #5

Can You Really Listen?

Danger signals can be faint, and
bad news travels slowly.

Kevin had plenty of role models for leadership in his early years. As a teenager, he looked up to his father, a captain in the navy who led a squadron of four hundred pilots. Keith Sharer was passionate about flying and leadership, often sharing his thoughts with his son. "If you're the captain of the squadron, you better be the best pilot," was one of his maxims. "Always have your hands on the throttles," he would say, a reminder to be prepared. So, young Kevin took to leadership early; in seventh grade, his Boy Scouts troop leader asked him to lead sixty other boys. He followed his father into military service, studying aeronautical engineering to become a pilot himself. He had to abandon that dream, however, when his eyesight didn't meet the standard for pilots, and instead he focused his energies on submarines.

There he met his next role model, Ken Strahm, commanding officer of the fast-attack nuclear submarine *USS Ray*. While they were docked in Norfolk, Virginia, Strahm and Kevin would often ride to work together. Kevin absorbed Strahm's leadership style—he was always calm, confident, and decisive, a contrast to the swashbuckling yellers who were more common in the military at the time. Strahm had high expectations for everyone, but he also delegated to his team and trusted them.

After eight years in the navy, Kevin joined General Electric at age thirty-six and began his quick rise up the career ladder, with a front-row seat to learn from Jack Welch. His boss was head of strategy and business development, so Kevin got many opportunities to brief Welch in person. As Kevin recalls, Welch was smart in every dimension—speed of processing, and an ability to conceptualize, recognize patterns, and ask penetrating questions. He also played well with a certain type of executive; if you were an introvert or unsure of yourself, it was not going to be a pleasant experience.

All these influences at key moments in Kevin's life reinforced certain core principles of leadership for him. The successful people he met and worked with were confident, made their expectations clear, and were an outsized presence. That command-and-control style came naturally to Kevin, and he was rewarded with regular promotions. "My mantra was, I'm in a hurry," he recalls. "And my approach was that I think I am the smartest guy in the room, and just let me prove that here in the first five minutes, because it won't take me any longer than that. I would even interrupt people and tell them what they were going to tell me to save us time, so we can get to the really important stuff, which is me telling them what to do. The phenomenal thing was that I got away with it. I was a quick study. It worked."

Until it didn't. After five years at GE and three at MCI, Kevin joined Amgen in 1992 as president and chief operating officer. He was named CEO in 2000, built a new leadership team, and set the company on a trajectory of rising revenue and profits. The company was on a roll, and magazine cover stories and other recognition followed, pushing Kevin into what, in hindsight, he calls the "ego danger zone." He was paying less attention and not probing enough—"I became intellectually lazy." The talk in the company, as a trusted lieutenant later informed him, was that you should avoid meeting with the boss after 3 p.m., because he became less engaged as the day wore on.

Then a crisis hit. Seven years into his CEO tenure at Amgen, a red-blood-cell stimulant called Epogen, which accounted for a third of Amgen's profits and was believed to be nearly free of side effects, was flagged in studies that suggested it caused a slightly higher risk of heart problems for patients at higher doses. The US Food and Drug Administration (FDA) ordered changes in how it was prescribed, which sharply lowered sales of Amgen's workhorse drug. As profits fell, Kevin ordered the first mass layoff in the company's history, cutting 14 percent of its staff. At first, he was angry, and blamed others for the debacle. "I was completely in denial," Kevin recalls. "I had become impatient and arrogant, and I assumed people were going to fix the problem. But in that crisis, I realized I was a horrible listener."

That epiphany came when he was sitting alone in a restaurant in Santa Monica, waiting for his daughter and her husband to join him for dinner. They were stuck in traffic, giving him time to reflect. He could no longer escape the hard truth that he had mishandled the Epogen crisis and started scribbling down what he had to own on the white paper tablecloth. The list quickly grew to more than a dozen critiques of himself, including, "I didn't really listen to the problem. I wasn't really engaged. I didn't make sure that our relationships with our regulator were strong. I assumed people were going to fix it, but I didn't give them clear guidance or set up proper follow-up processes."

From that day on, he resolved that he would work on becoming a better listener. Instead of thinking of eight things at once when he was meeting with people, he would be more present in the moment. Instead of approaching every conversation as a transactional exchange, cutting people off and telling them what to do, Kevin would start asking for more context and suggestions. He would listen not just to what someone was saying, but also watch for body-language clues about what somebody was holding back. As part of his reset, he sat down with his two key lieutenants and stunned them with an admission that he had to shoulder a lot of the blame for what went wrong, specifying where he had fallen short. He then created a regular cadence of surveys, conversations, and feedback mechanisms to open lines of communication inside and outside the company so that he could better hear distant warning signals as well as opportunities. He recognized that the art of listening for leaders is one part mindset—the discipline of pushing aside all distractions and judgments in the moment to listen purely for comprehension—and one part commitment to create systems and processes on all fronts to elevate the idea of "active listening" to one of hypervigilance.

"It's not just about listening to the person across the table from you," Kevin says. "Listening is actually being alert to the whole eco-system in which you operate. The signals come to you with varying intensity from varying sources, whether it was a comment from an FDA regulator, the board, the press, the anecdotes that you pick up inside the company. Can you listen to all the signals and separate the signal from the noise? That's not an easy thing to do because most of the communications that come to you are curated to have a pleasing tone, because the team wants to protect you from negative signals or issues that are emerging."

· · ·

You won't find a course on listening in many business schools, yet it is an essential skill for leaders to counteract the many powerful forces that can conspire to trap them in dangerous bubbles, lulling them into a false confidence that they really know what's happening in their organizations. And because problems rarely get better with age, the consequences of inaction grow over time, with results that can be catastrophic. Perhaps the most famous example of this phenomenon is the explosion of the Space Shuttle *Challenger* in 1986 due to faulty O-rings that failed to create a critical seal in cold weather. The com-mission that investigated the disaster leveled harsh criticism at NASA for "management isolation" by the leaders who were responsible for the design and production of the failed booster rockets. Companies fall into the same trap time and again (for example, Boeing and the 737 MAX safety issues), crippled by problems that somebody in the chain of command decided not to flag to their bosses because they feared being punished, or because they assumed they would be ignored or perhaps face pressure from colleagues not to make waves.

At the core of the challenge is a central paradox of the life of a senior leader, and particularly the CEO—they may have access to more lines of communication in the company than anybody else, yet the information flowing to them is more suspect and compromised than it is for everyone else. Warning signals are tamped down. Key facts are omitted. Data sets are given a positive topspin. When the leader asks questions, the default response is often a two thumbs-up, "Everything's great, boss!" Leaders who suspect they are not getting the full and complete picture can find themselves staring at the ceiling in the middle of the night, wondering, "How do I know what I need to know?" Answering this question often involves far more effort than leaders think. There are always dozens of emerging problems inside organizations, some of which have the potential to cripple the enterprise if left unchecked.

Yet leaders often trap themselves in information bubbles, a result of their confidence and outdated ideas about leadership. They believe, as Kevin did early in his career, that they are a step ahead of everyone else, confident that they know the answers and impatient to hear people out. Many senior executives still subscribe to the "lead, follow, or get out of the way" approach. And there is no arguing with the efficiency of this leadership style, at least in the short term. "Do this now" saves a lot more time than saying, "We have this challenge, so what are your thoughts on the best approach?" Some CEOs tell themselves that their leadership team is paid handsomely to do their jobs, and that includes handling problems so they don't splash up to their boss. In the book *Lights Out: Pride, Delusion, and the Fall of General Electric*, authors Thomas Gryta and Ted Mann describe how former CEO Jeff Immelt would say to subordinates who raised doubts about whether certain ambitious growth targets could be met: "Your people don't want it bad enough." At that point, the employee would stop communicating with the CEO, creating a phenomenon of "success theater," with results framed in ways to suggest apparent progress, thereby avoiding tough conversations about real problems. Such signals from the leader—and Immelt is hardly alone in this approach—conspire to shut down anyone from raising troubling questions or sharing bad news.

"The single defining characteristic of every underperforming company we went after was that the CEO had walled himself off from any kind of skepticism," said Nell Minow, who was a principal in the 1990s of shareholder-activist fund Lens, which took positions in roughly two dozen companies such as Sears, *Reader's Digest*, and Waste Management and then embarked on public campaigns to pressure the company's directors and leadership into taking action. "All those companies had CEOs who took an enormous number of steps to make sure that no one would ever question them or second-guess them," Minow added. "At one of the companies we were involved in, we talked to a number of employees who all used the exact same phrase—if you disagree with the boss, you get fired on the spot."

"We talked to a number of employees
who all used the exact same phrase—
if you disagree with the boss,
you get fired on the spot."

—Nell Minow, former principal, Lens

The perks and rarified air of a senior executive's life can be intoxicating and dangerous. While many leaders are fond of saying that they have an open-door policy, they often do not really mean it; the door may be open, but people quickly figure out that they can't just walk in. When they do meet with the boss, many employees come with a side agenda. Some are more subtle about it than others, but invariably they are trying to advance some personal cause, whether it's their own career ambitions (maybe by throwing a colleague under the bus) or to lobby for more resources. All these forces combine to create a formidable challenge for senior leaders to listen more effectively so that they have a clear understanding of all the signals within their organization, both good and bad. Breaking through the bubble requires intentional strategies, starting with an awareness that the bubble exists in the first place.

. . .

In the fifth season of *The Sopranos*, HBO's seminal series about a mobster and his family living in the New Jersey suburbs, there is a scene in which Tony Soprano, the mob boss and central character, is bickering with his wife, Carmela. They had recently separated and were arguing about some bills, including the cost of a new sound system for the media room in their house. He sarcastically asks whether it's for her and her "movie connoisseur friends." "At least I have friends," she snaps back. "What's that supposed to mean?" Tony demands. She tells him that the guys he hangs out with are his flunkies, not his friends, because they're on his payroll. "You're the boss. They're scared of you," she says, adding that it's their job to "laugh at your stupid jokes."

"Watch how funny your jokes get."

—Nell Minow, former principal, Lens

Tony storms off, but Carmela has planted the seed of doubt in his mind. Later in the episode, when he is playing poker with his crew, Tony decides to test her theory by telling an intentionally unfunny joke. "What do you get when you cross an accountant with a giant jet airplane?" he asks the group. "A *Boring* 747." His lieutenants burst into laughter, catching Tony by surprise, and the audience is treated to a slow-motion pan around the table, with close-ups of his men laughing uproariously and pointing at him as if he were a comedic genius. The camera returns to Tony's face, where his slow blink signals to the audience that he recognizes Carmela was right.

"Watch how funny your jokes get." It is the leadership rule that Minow heard from her longtime business partner, Bob Monks, when she stepped into her first big leadership role as president of Institutional Investor Services. "I must think about that three or four times a week," Minow said. "Not because I'm telling a joke and people are laughing, but because I need to remind myself constantly of the challenge that gets tougher and tougher as you get higher in the organization to get people to be honest with you."

So how do leaders break through the bubble? Here are some examples of how leaders set the tone and expectation for their employees to share unvarnished truths with them:

- When Bracken Darrell joined Logitech, the technology accessories company, in 2012, he encountered a culture where people were too nice, and they stood by as the company's performance suffered. So he articulated several values early on in his tenure, including what he considered the most important one: speaking up. "When people go through a tough time, as Logitech had for about four years, everybody's talking about problems," Darrell said. "But if nobody listens to them, they stop talking about problems, so you don't know what they are. The most dangerous thing is to be sitting in an office and nobody's telling you what's wrong. So I immediately started talking about speaking up and moving fast. I don't like being around people who are jerks, but I do want everybody to challenge everybody else."

- Kelly Grier of Ernst & Young told people they had a responsibility to keep her informed about what she needed to know. "If you haven't created a culture or an environment where people feel free to challenge you as the leader, you are in a very perilous and dangerous place, because you will have blind spots," she said. As she's moved into her past five leadership roles, she's said to everyone on her team, as well as to her board of directors, "You have a responsibility to help me actively work the blind spot. You've got to bring the truth forward. You've got to speak with candor. We have to have that level of trust."

"Hierarchy is a necessary evil of managing complexity, but it in no way has anything to do with respect that is owed to an individual."

—Mark Templeton, former President and CEO, Citrix Systems

- Mark Templeton, the former CEO of software company Citrix, adopted a framework to ensure his employees weren't intimidated by titles or rank. "You have to make sure you never confuse the hierarchy that you need for managing complexity with the respect that people deserve," he said. "Because that's where a lot of organizations go off track, by confusing respect and hierarchy, and thinking that low on hierarchy means low respect; high on the hierarchy means high respect. So hierarchy is a necessary evil of managing complexity, but it in no way has anything to do with respect that is owed to an individual. If you say that to everyone over and over and over, it allows people in the company to send me an email no matter what their title might be or to come up to me at any time and point out something—a great idea or a great problem or to seek advice or whatever."

- Penny Pritzker, the former US commerce secretary, would have a blunt first-day conversation with job candidates about the dangers of not sharing problems. "When we get close to saying we want to hire someone, I will talk to them about what could get them fired," she said. "If you want to get fired, here's what you need to do: first, lie, cheat, or steal. But the other thing that will get you fired is if you have a problem and you keep it to yourself. Problems are going to happen, and it's my job to help you with your problem. What I've learned is that the most troublesome people don't tell you 100 percent of the story and keep some facts to themselves. They just don't give you the full picture, and that's very worrisome to me. Oftentimes it's because they don't want to tell you the things you don't want to hear. You need to give them permission to give you bad news."

- Anand Chandrasekher, the CEO of Aira Technologies, a wireless systems company, asks his team to follow a simple rule: if they have bad news, they should text him. If it's good news, they should wait to share it with him in person. "The toughest thing in any organization is getting people to absolutely speak the truth," he said. "It's a human tendency to want to share only good news and to receive good news. If you can get a team and an organization not to be afraid of bad news, either receiving it or delivering it, then you can build an early-warning system. If you get bad news early, you can react faster, and that reaction time is precious."

- When he meets on occasion with groups of employees, Paul Kenward, the managing director of British Sugar, will ask them, "What are the things over the last five years that you've been really proud of that we've achieved at British Sugar?" After they answer, he then asks, "Now imagine we're together five years from now. What are we proud of now? What would you really have loved to have achieved, or for the business to have changed?" These questions make it easier for people to talk positively about a problem they're seeing today, Kenward said. "It's a simple approach, but it's clever," he added. "You have to ask people first about what they're proud to have achieved. People need to feel that they have made progress. It's difficult enough to make change happen. If you don't reflect on the fact that we are able to change things, people give up before they've started. And most organizations actually have changed quite a lot of things. You just have to help people realize that." One additional benefit of this approach is that it keeps the conversation focused on big ideas to improve the organization, thereby discouraging the griping over small stuff that sometimes creeps into all-hands Q&A sessions.

> ## "If you really want to know what's going on, you get out there and you listen to folks on the front lines."
>
> **—Susan Story, former CEO, American Water**

It's not enough to set the expectation that people need to speak up. Leaders have to invest the time and energy to walk the halls, to travel to their manufacturing plants or stores, to hold regular town-hall meetings (ideally with opportunities for employees to ask questions anonymously), and to meet with smaller groups of employees from different departments and ranks. Yes, that can be time consuming, but it is a core part of a leader's job. If they get stuck in an ivory-tower mindset, the gap between their perception and the reality of what's happening inside their company will grow, which can slow momentum and send top talent heading for the exits. For Susan Story, the former CEO of American Water, a utility company, a vivid memory from her childhood provides a constant reminder to get out of her office and meet with employees. "I remember when I was twelve years old, and my dad was a pipefitter," she said. "He was working on a big project, and he came home shaking his head because he had an idea that could save his employer a huge amount of money, but his supervisor wouldn't listen to him. And I remember thinking, 'What a dumb supervisor.' That stayed with me. If you really want to know what's going on, you get out there and you listen to folks on the front lines."

Meetings with broader employee groups are important opportunities to remind people of the strategy and to clear up any misconceptions during the Q&A session. But leaders also can use these sessions as their early-warning systems to detect problems, using effective lines of questioning to get people to share what's on their minds. When she was leading A+E Networks, Abbe Raven would regularly host small gatherings for breakfast, lunch, or coffee with employees at different levels. "My opening question was always: 'If I had been a CEO who came from the outside and you were meeting that CEO for the first time, what would the topics be that you would talk about? What should we change, and what shouldn't we change?'" She would also stop new employees in the hall after they had been there for a few months and ask them: "What is working for you here that you didn't have before? And is there something that you used to do at your old company that we should be doing?"

In those moments, in small groups or one-on-one meetings, leaders need to practice the core skills of listening to draw people out. Senior executives can find it challenging to be fully present when they have ten things on their minds at any moment, but it is a necessary discipline. It also means listening for understanding and withholding judgments. "You can't have an agenda," said Joel Peterson, the chairman of JetBlue Airways and founder of Peterson Partners, an investment firm. "When you have your own agenda when you're listening to someone, what you're doing is formulating your response rather than processing what the other person is saying. You have to really be at home with yourself. If you have these driving needs to show off or be heard or whatever, then that kind of overwhelms the process.

If you're really grounded and at home with yourself, then you can actually get in the other person's world, and I think that builds trust." A helpful acronym for leaders to keep in mind is WAIT, which stands for, "Why Am I Talking?" because anything a leader says can quickly overwhelm a discussion and make people shut down.

"When you have your own agenda when you're listening to someone, what you're doing is formulating your response rather than processing what the other person is saying."
—Joel Peterson, Chairman, JetBlue Airways

Becoming a better listener is more than a Post-it reminder to leaders, and it is not simply another task added to a leader's staggering list of responsibilities. It is a shift in mindset and requires building skills to solicit regular feedback. Consider the "listening ecosystem" that Kevin developed during his years at Amgen. He would get a quarterly report from his team on relevant news from competitors so that he could learn from the challenges they were facing, and then ask questions about how Amgen was positioned to address those issues. He broadened his network of sources inside the company, including the head of Amgen's relationship with the FDA, its chief regulator. He developed a structured set of questions for those meetings, asking his colleagues, "Are we meeting our commitments with the FDA? Is there anybody at the FDA who has a bad opinion of us? What's the next key event at the FDA? Is there anything else you want to tell me?" He had regular meetings with a vice president who was in charge of compliance to make sure Amgen's sales force toed the line by only talking with doctors about the clinical effects of Amgen's drugs and not what they could mean for the doctors' bottom lines. He developed relationships with factory managers and visited them often. He went on rides with his sales reps, asking them between sales calls about any concerns they might have.

Listening for danger signals is crucial, but it's just as important to listen for signals about opportunities. After Amgen had weathered the Epogen crisis and was delivering solid growth again, the stock was not moving, in part because the biopharma industry was out of favor. Amgen's leadership and its big shareholders believed the stock was seriously undervalued. During a long conversation, one of the largest investors asked Kevin why so many companies in the bio-pharmaceutical industry carried so little debt. Conventional wisdom suggested that they needed a fortress balance sheet to weather any storms of patent expirations or crises like the one Amgen had just lived through.

The shareholder's question had stuck, and Kevin later started play-ing with some back-of-the-envelope calculations about what it would cost, in that period of low interest rates, to borrow money and use it to buy back a significant share of the company's stock and still have plenty of rainy-day money. His team blanched at the idea, but Kevin persisted, and Amgen bought back much of the company at $60 a share, and it has risen more than fourfold since then. Soon, many other drug companies followed Amgen's move, which had started with a simple question from a shareholder. "The signal was unexpected, and it took my being open to it and willing to take a bit of a risk to act," he says. (This example is not meant to suggest stock buybacks are a panacea; they have drawn deserved criticism in many instances for accomplishing little more than draining cash reserves for short-lived stock bumps. But the fact that Amgen's stock has risen sharply since then suggests that the buyback was the right move at the right time.)

Other steps to build Kevin's listening ecosystem included asking his chief human resources officer, Brian McNamee, to do regular surveys of his leadership team about what they thought of his performance. The questions he asked on Kevin's behalf included: "What am I doing that you want me to keep doing? What are the things that I should either stop doing or significantly modify? What are the things that I should start doing or do a lot more of? Is there anything else you want to tell me?" To encourage candor, McNamee would take all the answers and synthesize them into a report for Kevin, who in turn would pass it along to the board members to discuss on their own (Kevin's CEO friends thought he was crazy to do this). On the annual survey of all Amgen employees, Kevin would include the question, "What do you think of the job that Kevin is doing?" with an open field for people to write in any additional comments about their perceptions of his performance. There were hundreds of responses, which Kevin would read at night, often with an adult beverage nearby to help him take in the sometimes-blunt feedback. For example, many shared that they felt Kevin tended to be a remote leader. So he committed to spending more time being visible in the company, including walking the halls, chatting with colleagues in the cafeteria, and holding more town-hall meetings.

"Creating listening systems is not just about passively accepting what comes your way," he says. "You have to create structures so that people know you want to hear what they have to say." That means acting on their best suggestions, and it means proving to people that you're listening to them. For example, after an important meeting or discussion with Amgen's board, Kevin would often write up a summary of the items that were discussed, acknowledge their input, document what he would do in terms of next steps, and send it to all the directors. "This proves you listened, you respect and understand what they said, and are clear on the action you're taking," he says. "They can then never claim you did not hear them. You also get to define the reality of what happened and are clear on next steps, giving them a chance to disagree or clarify their input."

On a regular basis, Kevin even recreated the kind of truth-telling moment for himself that he had at the Italian restaurant in Santa Monica after the Epogen crisis. "I would occasionally go off by myself and write down what reality really was in my view, not some sanitized version of it," he says. "What are the real issues we're facing? What I was always trying to do was get an understanding of reality—not my version of what I wish it were, not some fantasy, not some partial picture, but hardball reality." Ten years into his tenure as CEO, Kevin spent a weekend alone at a rented cottage on the California coast to write a kind of report card on his own performance over the last decade, including what he did well and could have done better, and what he needed to focus on to meet the company's challenges in the future. He shared that with his board of directors as well.

He also changed the way he listened, trying to be much more present and attuned to body language than he had been before the crisis. "It's like the scales had fallen from my eyes," Kevin recalls. "I understood that many of the behavioral patterns I had adopted for reasons of efficiency and decisiveness had in fact impeded listening. So I slowed down. I made sure I was ready to listen and made time to listen." He had designed his office to look like a living room and would always sit in chairs away from his desk for one-on-one meetings. "I wanted to create an environment where my direct reports trusted me that they could tell me bad news and they didn't feel like they'd get punished," he said. "You have to treat your direct reports as partners, not as subordinates. And partners can talk about tough issues together and come up with a collaborative best response. I had periodic conversations with them when I just asked, 'What's going on?' I wouldn't be rushed. I'd take the approach of a counselor and coach, not as a judge."

Leaders cannot take the signals from their organization at face value, and they must develop strategies to be able to answer a question that every senior executive has to be able to answer for themselves: How do you get a sense of the true nature of your organization and its dynamics and what it feels like to the people who work there? "If you just walk around and see a bunch of happy faces and say, gee, everybody looks happy to me, you're not listening, because the ecosystem is not designed to give you that information," Kevin says.

Leaders cannot survive or thrive until they learn that listening is a multidimensional practice that requires commitment and constant attention. It means turning the cliché of "no news is good news" on its head. No news is bad news, because that means that the distant warning signals of problems are not reaching you.

Test #6
Can You Handle a Crisis?

Avoid the predictable mistakes that trip up so many leaders.

We are writing these words in the summer of 2020, with the coronavirus crisis still holding the planet in a tight grip. In the United States, new records are set every day for the number of people who have contracted the virus, and worldwide the death toll from Covid-19 continues to grow. Trials are underway for promising vaccines, but nobody is expecting a solution until 2021, at the earliest, that will finally end this pandemic. It is the defining crisis of our time, drawing comparisons to the 1918 flu pandemic and the Great Depression, and prompting endless questions about what life will look like in the new normal on the other side. Is remote work here to stay? Is the grinding life of the road warrior over, now that people have realized that video calls are just as effective and far more efficient? What is the future of commercial real estate? Shopping malls? Higher education? Tourism?

> ## "It used to be that most of these levers were behind the scenes. They were operational. There were a couple of stakeholders who had big, loud voices, and leaders tended to focus on managing them. Today, everything is louder, and leaders must be attentive to more engaged stakeholders. That requires a pretty skillful hand."
>
> **—George Barrett, former Chairman and CEO, Cardinal Health**

For many senior executives, the crisis has been a profound new leadership challenge, particularly for those who have moved into management positions in the last twelve years, an unusually stable period since the financial crisis of 2008. But it's a safe bet that some other crisis is going to turn the world upside down over the next decade or so. Perhaps we should finally retire the phrase "once in a lifetime" that is often invoked to describe such events, because we seem to be packing more such crises into a single lifetime. When Covid-19 shifted overnight from a distant curiosity to a threat at our front doors in March 2020, it arguably marked the official start of the

VUCA era, an acronym coined by the US Army War College that stands for volatility, uncertainty, complexity, and ambiguity. What's next? Cyberattacks? A new flashpoint in the long-building climate crisis? Another deadly virus?

If uncertainty is the new certainty, then leaders must prepare for it, and not just for external crises that are the equivalent of a meteor strike that affects everyone, like Covid-19. Over the course of a long career, leaders can expect to face several crises that are specific to their organization, division, or team. Hackers may expose sensitive customer data. A software glitch could lead to safety hazards. A factory accident may injure employees and halt important production. A single employee's tweet could escalate into a social media backlash that damages the reputation of your organization. For all leaders, there is simply more to worry about, particularly as the lines between work and life have blurred, with corporations, rather than government, facing greater expectations to right more of society's wrongs. "The role is evolving, and it's going to require a different kind of intelligence and greater situational awareness," George Barrett, the former chief executive of Cardinal Health, said about CEOs, though the same is true for all leaders. "The job requires managing multiple levers. It used to be that most of these levers were behind the scenes. They were operational. There were a couple of stakeholders who had big, loud voices, and leaders tended to focus on managing them. Today, everything is louder, and leaders must be attentive to more engaged stakeholders. That requires a pretty skillful hand."

Leading through a crisis is a kind of final exam of all the tests that we've described in the previous chapters. If you've established a simple plan, fostered a strong culture, developed a cohesive team, and built an ecosystem to ensure you're hearing important signals, you're much more likely to better weather the next crisis. The middle of a crisis is not the time to start working on those foundations. Because when you're under tremendous pressure, with knots in your stomach that make clear thinking a challenge, you need to rely on muscle memory to navigate through the crisis. Your team will be looking to you, as the leader, to be calm, confident, and credible, and you cannot fake those qualities. They can come from painful lessons from surviving previous crises, but you can also learn them by understanding the predictable patterns of crises and what to do and not do based on the experience of others.

Our goal has been to provide a playbook that slows down the game to help you better understand the dynamics of different challenges and the leadership approaches that will put you in the best position to succeed. The particular challenge of leading in a crisis is to bring some predictability to moments of intense unpredictability and stress, when so much is on the line, including your own and your organization's reputations. Because of the very different nature of the two kinds of crises—an external shock, like Covid-19, versus a critical problem that emerges within the metaphorical four walls of your organization—we are going to examine them separately, sharing the lessons of leaders who have lived through each. Let's start with Covid-19, since it is the most current and urgent case study, and then we will discuss how to handle more homegrown crises.

. . .

There are so many unknowns about the coronavirus crisis—how many lives will be lost, when will a vaccine be found, how much damage will the economy ultimately suffer, how will the world be different on the other side. The path forward will almost certainly not be smooth or uniform, and it will be different for every organization and every industry. These existential questions about permanent changes to the way we live have made this crisis overwhelmingly difficult for so many leaders. In addition to trying to protect the viability of their business, they must now also worry about the mental health strain on employees who have been forced to work at home. When do they start bringing employees back to the workplace? How will they ensure it's safe? What if employees are reluctant to head back to the office? The financial crisis of 2008 seems so simple by comparison, as it was defined by just two overarching questions: How deep is the financial hole? How long will it take to get out of it?

Yet, for all the uncertainty and breadth and depth of the pain that the pandemic has caused, there are aspects of this pandemic that present a more straightforward leadership challenge than a crisis that is unique to your organization. After all, the Covid-19 threat is affecting everyone, and, aside from politicians and health officials whose actions and inactions are being scrutinized, the leaders of most organizations are not being blamed for it. The coronavirus has hit the pause button on the global economy, so the financial strain on companies is not seen as an indictment of strategies or the result of a misguided bet on a product or service. As with many externally driven crises, there is a sense that everyone is in this together, learning crisis management lessons.

Key themes emerged from dozens of conversations with leaders about the crisis. They will serve as important reminders when the next once-in-a-lifetime event arrives, probably within the next decade.

Show Up and Be Human

Surprisingly, not every leader shows up when a crisis hits, particularly when the time comes to make painful cost cuts (which Covid-19 has forced on many companies). David Reimer, CEO at Merryck, spent a dozen years earlier in his career at Drake Beam Morin, a consulting firm that helps companies with restructurings and layoffs. Most leaders retreated to the shadows during moments of crisis, he said. Reimer recalled,

> "In these moments, it's important for leaders to show their human side."
> —Tim Ryan, US Chairman and Senior Partner, PwC

They'd make an announcement about a restructuring, but then sort of vanish from the internal spotlight for a while. Then there were CEOs who were pretty good about at least getting the message out on a regular basis through town halls. But they also stayed at arm's length, particularly once they'd announced a layoff. And then there were CEOs who would actually check on the people who'd been laid off to see how they were doing. So with some CEOs, their stated values literally didn't end with your layoff notice, to some degree. People who stayed felt differently about the place because they knew that even though it wasn't employment for life, there was a psychological contract that would extend beyond their formal association with the organization.

Leaders need to be more visible than usual during times of crisis, because they need to set the tone through their words, deeds, and body language. Even in more stable times, leaders are always "over-read," meaning their employees analyze every furrowed brow, hunched shoulder, or stray comment for hidden meaning. But leaders can also use that scrutiny to send clear signals that any cuts are being made with a deep appreciation of their emotional and financial toll on the people they are letting go.

For example, Arne Sorenson, the CEO of Marriott International, won widespread admiration for an emotional six-minute video he posted in March 2020 in which he talked about the steep losses the company was suffering (he explained that he would be forgoing his salary for the balance of the year, and that his executive team's pay was being cut by 50 percent). He acknowledged that his team had misgivings about him delivering the message on video, where everybody could see the effects of his treatments for pancreatic cancer, including his "new bald look," as he said, and weight loss that made his suit look a couple of sizes too big. "I can tell you that I have never had a more difficult moment than this one," Sorenson says into the camera, visibly choking up. "There is simply nothing worse than telling highly valued associates—people who are the very heart of this company—that their roles are being impacted by events completely outside of their control."[1]

Employees want a confident leader, but they also want to see their human side. Tim Ryan, the US chairman and senior partner of PwC, was on one of his weekly webcasts with tens of thousands of PwC employees soon after the pandemic started when he shared with everyone that his family—he had six kids at home—had had their own blowup moment the previous Friday night. Everyone was dealing with the new stresses and strains of being quarantined and wondering if others were faring better. "In these moments, it's important for leaders to show their human side, and that you're not some superhuman CEO," Ryan said. "It was therapeutic to share, and it was therapeutic for our people to realize that 'I'm not the only one.' I probably got three hundred emails from people sharing their own blowup moments."

Capitalize on the Urgency

Imagine someone on the leadership team of a global company raising this question months before the coronavirus crisis started—"What would it take to get everyone able to work at home?" The team likely would have laughed off this suggestion as unrealistic, but if the team went ahead to explore the idea, here is probably what would have happened: the team would have formed committees, which in turn would have raised all sorts of concerns about the technical, legal, and HR challenges that such a shift would present. Eighteen months would likely pass before the committees concluded that it couldn't be done. Yet when Covid-19 left them no other choice, companies figured out how to get all their office workers set up at home virtually overnight.

Many of the core business skills that companies typically struggle with—prioritization, speed of decision making, and innovation—become much easier in a crisis. Sharon Daniels, the CEO of Arria NLG, an artificial intelligence firm that turns data into natural language, said that once the pandemic started she began each day's team meeting with a simple question to help everyone prioritize: "What's our focus today?" She added, "In the first week of the crisis, I said, 'We're not going to try to do everything. We're going to focus on the areas where we know we're going to have an impact, and it's OK that some of the other initiatives are going to take a backseat.' As it turns out, everything's moving forward. But it took the mental pressure off of people."

At ServiceNow, Pat Wadors said she saw more agility and more freedom to be "perfectly imperfect" at the company after the crisis hit. Innovations moved from idea to execution in just a week or two. They were introduced into the market, and customer feedback helped improve them. That's how it's supposed to work but often doesn't. "We're all in this awkward, wonky state, and so forgiveness has never been higher," she said. "We're not as worried about the polished output."

Give a room full of executives enough time, and they can easily come up with a long list of reasons *not* to do something. But in a crisis, there is less time to think and an urgency to act. For many companies, the question has become, how can we hold on to this way of doing business once we emerge from the crisis?

Embrace the Ambiguity

As a leader, how do you acknowledge the grim realities yet also be confident and inspiring? How do you understand and accommodate the emotional strain on people precisely when you need to hold them accountable to do their very best work? That starts with a foundation of trust. Employees have to know that you're giving them accurate information, including what you know and don't know. People have sharp antennae and will pick up on any spin. Then it becomes a matter of sensing the right approach for any given moment.

John Riccitiello, the CEO of Unity Technologies, a video game software company, said:

> It's an interesting balance. At one level, I want people to put their health and their family first. I tell everybody to also make dispensation for the people on your team. There might be single parents at home and they've got three kids bopping around who used to be in school. They're going to have a hard time, so make room for who they are. Make room for those who can't

quite contribute like they did before. On the other hand, every one of our employees has the majority of their net worth in our stock. It's important for them to know that we're strong, that they have a great job while this is happening, and they will have a great job when this is over. But they need to see the blemishes too.

Many senior executives say that the ability to embrace ambiguity has become the single most important skill that they now look for in their talent pipeline. The question is not about the right approach to leading in a crisis, but about matching the response to the situation at hand. These are gut calls.

Barbara Khouri, a veteran of six turnarounds over her career, said:

One minute you have to be calm to help everyone else calm down, but the next minute you have to be excited to help inspire people. One minute you have to empower people to be creative and try things on their own, and the next minute you've got to instill discipline and say, "This is what we're going to do, and everybody has to line up." You have to know when to laugh and when to take things seriously. In turnarounds, you need more prioritizing, more connection with others, more humanity, more trust, more communication, more clarity, more transparency, and more willingness to be there for people. But there is also less of a need for perfection and for having all the data before you make a decision.

Reimagine Your Organization

A crisis creates a rare opportunity to revisit long-standing assumptions about your organization. Ideas that may have seemed impossible to tackle are suddenly on the table. Pam Fields, who has been hired by more than a dozen companies to help lead their turnaround efforts, said crises create a rare opportunity for leadership teams to ask themselves a series of questions: If we were building the company today from scratch, what would we do differently? And once we get beyond this crisis, where would we want to be a year from now, three years from now, and what resources would be required to get us there? What are the momentum killers that would prevent us from getting there? Fields said:

> Once you have that framing architecture, it becomes a bit easier to begin asking and answering these hard questions. Maybe, for example, you want to be less dependent on brick-and-mortar retailers and shift to more of a direct-to-consumer model. Then you can go to the rank and file and explain it. You can say, "Here's where we are, here's where we want to be, here's how we are going to get there and the resources that are required." The four-part framework helps people understand the next step, whether you're in a crisis or not.
>
> Those of us who have lived through previous financial crises or other upheavals in the marketplace know that they end and there's a new normal that emerges out of it. So the question is,

what is that new normal going to be? How would you reimagine your company if you were starting it now, based on what you think the new normal will be once the crisis ends?

"How would you reimagine your company if you were starting it now, based on what you think the new normal will be once the crisis ends?"

—Pam Fields, executive mentor, Merryck & Co.

In crises like this, it is understandable and very human to feel overwhelmed and even a sense of loss over the plans that were in place before the coronavirus hit. Indeed, a post by Scott Berinato on hbr.org on March 23, 2020, titled "That Discomfort You're Feeling Is Grief" became its most-viewed online article in the magazine's history. The test for leaders is to shift their own and their organization's focus from what could have been to what might be. It is the mindset that defines successful entrepreneurs and great leaders. With the right balance of imagination and realism, *everything* can be an opportunity. Employees need to be reminded of that sometimes. It's hard to beat the story about Roger Bannister becoming the first person to run a mile in less than four minutes that Anand Chandrasekher of Aira Technologies shares with employees. Sports are sometimes overused as an analogy for business, but this is a powerful and concrete example of how people can sometimes limit their own thinking about what is possible, particularly at times when they feel as if the walls are closing in around them. Chandrasekher said:

> For a hundred years, people believed that it was not possible to run fast enough to break a four-minute mile. Even medical journals argued that it was a physical impossibility because of the strain it would put on a runner's heart. Bannister took up the challenge, as did an American, Wes Santee and an Australian, John Landy. Bannister finally broke it in 1954, and here's the punch line: Many more people broke the four-minute mile in the years that followed.

"Our job as managers and leaders is to create that belief around what's possible, so everyone stays focused. That's what humanity is based on. We effectively live on hope."

—Anand Chandrasekher, founder and CEO, Aira Technologies

For me, that is a fantastic example of how belief, not ability, can hold people back. It wasn't that man couldn't run a four-minute mile; it was that we couldn't imagine ourselves doing it. In periods of uncertainty, failure of imagination and belief will hold us back. Our job as managers and leaders is to create that belief around what's possible, so everyone stays focused. That's what humanity is based on. We effectively live on hope.

. . .

In crises like the pandemic, leaders can take some comfort in the fact that they are not alone. They did not cause the problem, and they are given some benefit of the doubt that they are doing their best to navigate the organization through it. There is real risk, both to the financial well-being of the enterprise and to the health and safety of employees, but the risk is depersonalized.

Internal crises are different. When a crisis flares up in a leader's organization, or even in their division, department, or team, the spotlight is harsher and less forgiving. You are going to feel very much alone, with your reputation, job, and even career prospects suddenly in jeopardy. The benefit of the doubt you get during a pandemic or global financial crisis isn't there. Instead, there's likely to be a presumption of guilt and little patience for nuanced explanations. People will judge you in ways that may be unfair, and they will impute motivations to your actions that have no basis in reality. Time will feel compressed, limiting your options and freedom to act. There may be a root cause of the problem that you don't fully understand yourself, and you will need time to figure it out. These are the corporate crises that spring up with surprising regularity, such as the thousands of Wells Fargo employees who opened bank accounts and applied for credit cards on behalf of customers who never authorized them to do so. Or the lapses at Boeing that led to the deadly crashes of its 737 MAX aircraft. Or the Deepwater Horizon oil spill in the Gulf of Mexico in 2010. And for every scandal that garners intense media attention for months on end, there are countless other lesser-known crises inside organizations that all have the same effect of making the leader feel as if they are in an interrogation room, being pummeled with questions and table-pounding demands for quick answers.

In those early moments, most leaders make the most common and regrettable mistake in managing an internal crisis. They say something they do not know, usually in the spirit of wanting to minimize the severity of the problem. After an explosion on the Deepwater Horizon drilling rig that killed eleven workers, Tony Hayward, the CEO of BP, which had chartered the rig from Transocean, tried at first to distance the company from the disaster. "This was not our accident," Hayward said two weeks after the explosion. "This was not our drilling rig. This was Transocean's rig. Their systems. Their people. Their equipment." Eleven days later, with tens of thousands of barrels of oil a day shooting out of the seafloor, Hayward said, "The Gulf of Mexico is a very big ocean. The amount of volume of oil and dispersant we are putting into it is tiny in relation to the total water volume." In all about 5 million gallons of oil leaked from the well, making it the world's largest accidental spill. Four days later, Hayward said, "I think the environmental impact of this disaster is likely to have been very, very modest." He would go on to make more gaffes that would hasten his departure from the job, including an interview in which he said, "We're sorry for the massive disruption it's caused to their lives. There's no one who wants this over more than I do. I'd like my life back."[2]

Such crises provide steady work for people like Tom Strickland, who over the course of a long career—as an attorney, politician, and government official—has found himself in the center of a remarkable number of high-profile crises. He was, for example, chief of staff to Ken Salazar, the Interior Department secretary, when the Deepwater crisis occurred. Earlier in his career, he was about to be sworn in as the new US attorney for Colorado when Columbine High School seniors Eric Harris and Dylan Klebold killed twelve students and one teacher, so Strickland spent his first day on the job at the crime scene and holding a press conference in front of hundreds of reporters with Janet Reno, the attorney general of the Clinton administration.

> ## "The single biggest mistake that leaders make in dealing with a crisis is that they go beyond what they really know."
> **—Tom Strickland, Partner, WilmerHale**

During his career, he was brought in as general counsel to help clean up the stock-option backdating scandal at UnitedHealth and has been an adviser on other prominent crises, including the implosion of Theranos after serious questions were raised about its blood-testing science; the Target data breach that the company initially said affected 40 million customers and then raised the number to as many as 110 million customers; allegations that the University of Colorado used sex and alcohol to help recruit high school athletes; and the rape of a Vanderbilt student by four of the university's football players. As an attorney now for WilmerHale, he spends much of his time advising boards of directors and chief executives on how to handle a crisis. He sees clear patterns in the responses. "It's really astonishing," he said, "how the same mistakes get made time and again."

The most common problem he encounters is denial. Leaders can't quite believe that something happened on their watch, and they start circling the wagons to protect themselves and their company. Then they engage in wishful thinking that the problem is not such a big deal. But just one false note during this time will squander the most precious resource you have—your credibility—which is almost impossible to get back. "Human nature being what it is, people don't really like to apologize or accept responsibility," Strickland said. "That's why it's important to just be humble about what you know and what you don't know. The single biggest mistake that leaders make in dealing with a crisis is that they go beyond what they really know."

From there, the overarching script is to commit to getting to the bottom of the problem; be transparent and communicate with all the organization's key constituents such as customers, regulators, employees, the board of directors, and the media; and promise to take action, including holding people accountable, to ensure a similar crisis won't occur again. Strickland's frequent advice to leaders in the middle of a crisis is to accept the facts for what they are: "Whatever happened up to this moment in time is set in stone. We're going to find out what the facts are, and how you deal with those facts going forward is all that you can control right now. As uncomfortable as the facts may be, you're going to have to deal with them. It's like going to the doctor. You don't want to hear bad news, but it's worse not know-ing what's wrong with you."

"It's like going to the doctor. You don't want to hear bad news, but it's worse not knowing what's wrong with you."
—Tom Strickland, Partner, WilmerHale

In the previous chapter, we shared the story of Kevin's realization that he needed to be a much better listener after a crisis at Amgen over its Epogen drug and the steps he took to be more attuned to distant warning signals. A closer look at those events also provides a case study in crisis management—and mismanagement, at first—bringing to life many of the themes that Strickland described.

Kevin fell into the same trap that many leaders find themselves in early on in a crisis: denial. In 2007, when Kevin was seven years into his tenure as CEO, everything seemed to be breaking Amgen's way. It was the leading biotech company, it had recently passed $100 billion in market capitalization, and Kevin had appeared on the cover of *Forbes* magazine when Amgen was named "Company of the Year." "I was feeling pretty good about yours truly and the company," he said. Epogen played a big role in the company's success. The drug, mostly used by people on dialysis, is a genetically engineered ver-sion of erythropoietin, or EPO, a protein made in the kidneys to stimulate production of oxygen-carrying red blood cells. It had been approved more than fifteen years earlier and had been used by millions of patients. It brought in billions of dollars in revenue and generated an outsized share of Amgen's profits. Because of Amgen's success, the company drew scrutiny from regulators and criticism from competitors, but Kevin came to see it as predictable background noise—"chirping from the sidelines," as he called it.

But in early 2007, those chirps started sounding more like alarms. At an FDA hearing, a regulator called out Amgen for not living up to a commitment it made nine years earlier to do certain follow-up tests on Epogen. The *New York Times* published a front-page story about Amgen's pricing structure for Epogen and Aranesp, a similar drug used for cancer patients, saying that the company was paying out rich rewards to doctors to prescribe the drugs. The FDA, based on a new study by a scientist in Denmark about the effects of Epogen at high dosages, required the company to add a warning label to the drug. The narrative around the company quickly shifted, captured in the first two paragraphs of another article in the *New York Times*: "Until recently, Amgen was still considered one of the biggest success stories of the fast-growing biotechnology industry. Now some analysts are comparing it to a lumbering, stumbling pharmaceutical giant that leans too heavily on an aging product portfolio. A series of setbacks, some unexpected and some perhaps self-inflicted, pose the greatest challenge in the company's previously charmed 27-year history."[3]

With the credibility of Amgen and its products at risk, and with the potential loss of billions in revenue and profit, denial was no longer an option, and Kevin got over his defensiveness. He gave a full briefing to his board and formed a task force to help regain control of the narrative. "We've got to act," he told the group. "Amgen is a science-based company, but the world does not always act that way."

Even though he was saying to his team in no uncertain terms that the company was in the middle of a crisis, not everyone in the group agreed with him, arguing that the tough coverage in the media would soon be old news, the study out of Denmark was raising red flags about dosage levels that were unrealistically high, and the FDA was just doing its usual saber-rattling. The scientists at Amgen took the scrutiny as an affront to their credibility, arguing that the language of science was being perverted for political reasons. And there was finger-pointing within the company, with scientists and salespeople blaming each other for the problems.

That's when Kevin hit his low point and realized that he had to hold himself accountable for Amgen's problems, and that he could no longer outsource the job of solving the current crisis to his team. He had to own it. "The true 'aha' moment was me recognizing what had happened and saying to myself, 'Kevin, you've got a real problem here. You haven't managed this problem well, and you're blaming a bunch of other people, and the real core issue is you. And you have not been sufficiently engaged. You have accepted all these good results when you never asked the real, hard, penetrating questions. You have not been objective.'"

He no longer questioned the facts, only what he would do about them. Though Amgen could marshal scientific arguments about why the FDA was overreacting, he realized there was little hope of changing the regulators' minds. From now on, the company would fully cooperate with the FDA. He accepted the inevitable financial hit that the company was going to take from falling sales and met in person with each of the company's biggest shareholders about the likely impact. He announced the first big layoff in the company's history and took other measures to lower Amgen's cost structure. He met with frontline employees—with those who were dealing directly with the FDA to better understand the points of tension, with staff on the operations side to build his own models to forecast the company's financial future, and with salespeople to hear the feedback they were getting from doctors. Kevin's mantra to investors and employees was, "We're going to be stronger coming out of this than we were going into it."

Perhaps the biggest shift was how the company was going to manage its relationship with the FDA. Amgen grew the team that managed the company's relationship with regulators and made sure the FDA had more access to Amgen's leadership team if it wanted to flag any concerns. In hindsight, Amgen's problems could be traced back to a kind of scientific arrogance—that it was different from other pharmaceutical companies, and that it knew more than the FDA. "Instead of viewing the agency as something to be tolerated, like the Department of Motor Vehicles, we changed to make sure that we brought a real institutional respect to all our dealings with them," Kevin recalls. "These are good people with a darn tough job, and they represent the American people. We've got to accept what reality is."

. . .

The playbook for leading through a crisis is not particularly complex. But putting it into practice when you're in the middle of a crisis is much harder, and the lessons are easily forgotten in the moment, when you can feel as overwhelmed as if you're trying to sail a small boat in a hurricane, struggling to remember the handful of sailing fundamentals to minimize the danger of being capsized. In those moments, there is little to no margin for error, and it can be hard to recover from early mistakes. In his consulting work, Kevin will occasionally get calls from clients who suddenly find themselves in the middle of a storm, asking for help. He will then walk them through his five critical pieces of advice. These are the fundamentals, and you have to get them right if you want to navigate a crisis successfully:

Understand the facts. In some cases, determining the precise cause of the crisis can be difficult. The facts may be hard to get and even harder to understand. Talk to those closest to the action, not their managers. Develop a hypothesis early on, with input from your team, about what has happened and why, and then modify as more facts emerge. Fight the powerful emotions of denial and wishful thinking and focus on what is known and not known.

Act fast. Who is affected by the crisis in the short term and possibly in the long term? What immediate steps can you take to mitigate the effects of the crisis or take care of those affected? Who needs to be briefed immediately? Is your presence at the scene of the crisis helpful or necessary? Understand the narrative emerging on social media and other platforms about your crisis.

Communicate widely. Accuracy is paramount; never say something you do not know to be true. Be humble and open about what you know at the moment, with a commitment to learn more and share new facts as they emerge. Build a shared understanding of the crisis with your team, the broader company, and the board. Reach out to key stakeholders, including shareholders, regulators, and customers.

Fix the root cause of the problem. Once you've managed any immediate fallout of the crisis, then it's time to focus on the underlying problem that led to the crisis. Often it is not a single event or mistake, but rather a series of lapses or consequences of subtle cultural signals about what matters. Examine the management processes in place so that you are clear on what is encouraged, tolerated, and not tolerated in your organization, and make any necessary changes so that you can sleep well at night, knowing that there is unlikely to be a replay of the same crisis.

Stay calm and project confidence. Your crisis may well feel like a direct assault on your reputation and a dismissal of all the good work you've done before the crisis hit. You will feel as if you've been hauled into a small, windowless room, with bosses and key stakeholders demanding answers and doubting every word you say. You may reach out for help and then hear conflicting advice, exacerbating the feeling of being alone. But you have to stay calm, focus on the facts, and move forward with confidence and humility.

Crises are a brutal test of leadership, and many executives don't survive them. Any weaknesses in your organization will be exposed and magnified. Your ability to handle a crisis will be a direct result of how you led before the crisis, and by how well you established your reputation as a trustworthy leader. That trust is inevitably eroded and even broken by a crisis. But know that if you handle the crisis properly, you and your organization will come out of it stronger.

Test #7

Can You Master the Inner Game of Leadership?

The conflicting demands and challenges must be managed.

Niki Leondakis, a veteran hotel-industry CEO, started managing people in college when she was promoted from waiter to shift supervisor at a restaurant called the Hungry U near the University of Massachusetts. She took the job seriously, but in that role, as well as in her first management job out of college, she made a common mistake of many young leaders: she was too friendly with the people she was managing and had to learn the appropriate boundaries and necessary distance that managers have to keep from their teams. "I think people fall into one of two camps," she said. "Very few people become a supervisor or a boss for the first time and know exactly where the right balance is. Both with myself and all the young managers I see, people seem to swing to one end of the pendulum or the other—overzealous with power or, 'I'm everybody's friend, and I want them to like me, and if they like me, maybe they'll do what I ask and then it'll be easier.'"

As she started advancing in her career, she adopted a more rigid and authoritarian style that she saw many men use, thinking that their approach was what successful leadership looked like. "That was in the early eighties," she recalled. "For women in general at that time, we all thought that to be successful or to be considered equal, you tried to really dress like men, act like men, and ensure people knew you were tough-minded and could make the tough calls and be decisive." But then a moment arrived when she recognized that she had swung the pendulum too far. She had to discipline someone on her team she liked and admired, and Leondakis's boss could tell she was struggling with how to have the conversation. Her advice: Tap into who you are and relate to her with compassion.

> "It took me a good ten years before I really found my center and learned how to be true to my values."
>
> —Niki Leondakis, CEO, CorePower Yoga

"That was sort of an epiphany for me," Leondakis said. "I thought that being tough-minded and decisive and all those qualities and traits that I thought I was supposed to exhibit meant that I couldn't show compassion. It was just a different experience for me to relate to this person with compassion and accountability at the same time and balance the two. From that point on, I became aware that there was this balance I could strike with being myself, being compassionate and holding people accountable. They were not mutually exclusive. Looking back, it took me a good ten years before I really found my center and learned how to be true to my values."

. . .

To take on the challenge of becoming an effective leader means signing up for the many long and steep learning curves that we have explored in the previous chapters—learning how to write and communicate a simple plan, build cultures and high-performing teams, drive change, create systems for listening, and manage crises. These are the tests that—through our lived experience, mentoring senior executives and interviews with hundreds of leaders—we have come to appreciate are the critical reasons why leaders succeed or fail in their roles. Our focus in the book thus far has been on what leaders must *do* to be effective; in this final chapter, we will shift the focus to the inner game of leadership and how leaders must *be*. Get this right—and find the metaphorical balance point that Leondakis and many other leaders described—and you will be far more effective in all the previous challenges. Getting it wrong won't necessarily derail you as a leader, but it will mean the job will exact a much higher toll on you emotionally and physically, and spill over into other aspects of your life.

Though many people are loath to admit it, except to perhaps friends, family, and trusted confidants, leadership is hellishly difficult. Faced with the ever-shifting variables of leadership, people understandably latch on to one approach, telling themselves that they have developed their own leadership style and that others need to accommodate it. But anyone who goes into a leadership position with a brute-force, do-this-my-way leadership style will soon be frustrated that the world is not bending to their will. Insecure in the shades of gray and contradictions of leadership, they harden their approach and become the terrible managers that everyone hates because they don't listen, they're uncaring, and they're short-tempered with anyone who doesn't give them what they want. Their approach may work in certain situations, but not most, and they will quickly lose their most talented employees.

> "The ones I'm most impressed with do not seem packaged. They have this sense of peace, this self-awareness, that says, 'I understand who I am.'"
> —James Hackett, former President and CEO, Ford Motor Company

But then there are other leaders who seem preternaturally clear-eyed, calm, and confident. It's not that they think they have all the answers; they often are the first to admit that they don't. But as they describe their approach to leadership and key lessons learned, it becomes clear that, like Leondakis, they have spent many years working through different approaches to arrive at a balance point that resolves the core challenges of leadership, so that they understand what it means to be a leader.

James Hackett learned this important lesson when he took over as CEO of the office furniture company Steelcase at the young age of thirty-nine, the start of a nearly two-decade run in that role. During that time, he was widely credited with turning around its corporate culture and spotting early the trend of shifting from cubicle environments to more open work environments. Shortly after becoming CEO, he was introduced to Bill Marriott, whose tenure as CEO of Marriott International ultimately spanned four decades. Hackett, who later ran Ford Motor Company for three years, recalled:

> As we were talking about strategy, I remember being struck by the look in his eyes as he talked. I understood in that moment that he knew who he was. I wanted to have that quality as a leader, where it's really clear who you are and what you stand for. On my flight home, I was looking out the window. I had been struggling for six or seven months about this notion of identity. What does a CEO look like and feel like? What's the texture of what you're supposed to be? And I understood from seeing Bill Marriott's eyes that you have to be who you are. Since then, because of the business we're in of selling office furniture, I've met just about every CEO who runs a big company.

The ones I'm most impressed with do not seem packaged.
They have this sense of peace, this self-awareness, that says,
"I understand who I am."

. . .

What does it take to reach that level of comfort and self-awareness?
Experience is the best teacher, of course. But our goal throughout
has been to share the hard-earned lessons and insights of hundreds
of leaders so that you can move faster and further along your leadership learning curve than you would on your own. Our overarching
framework to mastering the inner game of leadership is to embrace
leadership as a series of paradoxes.

We've mentioned some already, and we will discuss others here.
But understanding leadership as a series of contradictions is the first
step to making sense of all the whiplash-inducing advice you will
find in this field. For every expert who urges you to "lead from the
front," you can find another who insists that the best approach is
to "lead from behind." Or that confidence is key—"Never let them
see you sweat"—except when you should be vulnerable. When taking on a new leadership role, many argue, you should make quick
decisions to show urgency and impact. Others counsel patience, in
order to listen and really understand the root issues. The danger,
as we mentioned previously, lies in slavishly following any one-size-
fits-all approach. It's better to understand that the thorniest aspects
of leadership are hard because they are paradoxical. Is it this or is it
that? The answer is often both. What's needed is to flex one way or

the other depending on the subtleties of the situation. Every one-on-one interaction, every team meeting, requires a different approach to suit the moment, whether it's to push or hang back, to be demanding or understanding, to project brash optimism or acknowledge sobering challenges. Such moments, in a sense, are like skiing—you have to know the balance point, constantly adjusting and leaning in different directions as conditions and terrains require.

Consider, for example, the balancing act that Satya Nadella faced when he was named CEO of Microsoft in early 2014. He was a twenty-two-year insider with a mandate to be a change agent. The board needed him to make a sharp break from the past, particularly from all the cultural momentum killers that had made Microsoft slow and siloed, and that had weighed on the stock for more than a dozen years. Yet he would have to signal the need for a fresh start while working for a board of directors that included the two former CEOs of Microsoft, Bill Gates and Steve Ballmer, whose leadership helped create some of the problems that Nadella had to fix. Could he honor the past while making the case for drastic change?

Nadella, it turned out, had a deft touch for navigating such challenges. At his first big all-hands staff meeting, with Gates and Ballmer looking on, Nadella sent an important signal with his very first words: "Our industry does not respect tradition. What it respects is innovation."[1] And to help tap into its history of innovation, Nadella asked Gates to help him by spending more time in a technical advisory role. "One of the fantastic things that only Bill can do inside this campus is to get everybody energized to bring their 'A' game,"

Nadella said in his first month on the job. From there, Microsoft began its steady march to a trillion-dollar valuation, with its stock rising from $38 a share to more than $200 at the time of this writing. Nadella is in the small club of successful CEOs—Bob Iger of Disney is a member as well—who have shown that it is possible to be both an insider and a change agent.

We've mentioned a few other paradoxes of leadership in previous chapters, including the need to deliberately disrupt the way you are doing business to prepare for tomorrow, even as you're optimizing the way you're running your business today. Here are seven other paradoxes that are hallmarks of a leader's life and must be mastered to improve your chances of making good decisions and effectively leading the people who are relying on you.

Be Confident *and* Humble

As a leader, you have to have a clear vision, because the organization and all its stakeholders need you to inspire confidence. And confidence, in its healthiest manifestation of being authentic and credible, stems from a track record of demonstrating good judgment and engendering confidence in others. However, confidence cannot morph into arrogance, and the best safeguard is humility—acknowledging to your team that any ambitious effort is going to be difficult and will carry risks and the possibility of failure.

"One problem is people who are always overly optimistic and overconfident," said John W. Rogers Jr., the founder and co-CEO of

Ariel Investments. "You want people who are appropriately humble, open to explaining their mistakes, and not always creating the sense that they have all the answers. You want people who are open and honest about their strengths and their weaknesses personally, and the strengths and weaknesses of the organization, and are not always seeing everything through rose-colored glasses."

Be Urgent *and* Patient

Leaders who understand this paradox spend their time in ways that reflect the balancing act between now, soon, and later. It requires continuous fine-tuning of speed and being able to live with the fact that you will get it right one day and wrong the next. It means recognizing the need to slow down, bring people along by sharing context and rationales, and make sure there are proper processes and resources in place, even if you as the leader are feeling the weight of the world to achieve some target quickly. Move too slowly, however, and a competitor will blow past you.

"Your strength can really be a weakness at some point in your career," said Carla Cooper, the former CEO of Daymon Worldwide, a retail consultancy. "I embraced this idea of getting things done through other people and figuring out how to counsel associates so that they can motivate themselves, but it takes a lot of time and patience. So my patience is seen sometimes as being not aggressive or forceful enough about telling the team what to do. I constantly struggle with the balance of being patient and, on the other hand, saying,

'Here's the mountain, here's where we're going, here's what I need you to do, and here's why I need you to do it.' The balance is where the magic is."

Be Compassionate *and* Demanding

Leaders set a high bar for expectations. But those demands for exceptional performance have to be balanced with a sense of compassion and understanding that their team is made up of human beings. People do their best work when they are treated more like volunteers than mercenaries. Everybody is struggling with something in their lives—an ailing parent, a child having difficulties at school, a marriage under strain—and there are moments when understanding and appreciation are more important than a tough conversation about meeting next quarter's target. Compassion isn't about being soft; it's about acknowledging that we are all human. The tricky balance for leaders is to know when to push and when to be empathic.

Lucien Alziari, the chief human resources officer at Prudential Financial, captures this paradox in an approach he uses to give feedback to his team. "I tell them right up front, look, I grew up with tough love and you're going to experience tough love," Alziari said. "It's really important that you remember both sides of that phrase because if you're just experiencing tough, it's going to feel like the dark side of the moon. But know that I've got your best interest at heart and the only reason I'm doing this is because I believe in you and I want you to be even better than you are."

Be Optimistic *and* Realistic

Leaders are expected to be optimistic and to build energy, enthusiasm, and passion for the ambitious goals that they've laid out for the organization. The balancing act for leaders is to share the risks, build contingency plans, and put everyone on high alert that the plan may not play out as expected, yet also create a wide landing zone for success. How transparent should you be about the business challenges you're facing? You want to keep people inspired and focused on the long-term goal, but if you share too many of the storm clouds, people may start thinking they should look for another job. On the other hand, your staff shouldn't be blindsided by bad news, and sharing a challenge will invite them in to help. The best approach is to let people know about the big challenges (ideally paired with a plan for addressing them) while not overwhelming them. Chris Barbin, the former CEO of Appirio, an information technology company, said:

> I don't think a lot of leaders are great at true transparency. Transparency can mean, if things aren't going well financially, just being blunt and direct about it. The only way a team can get out of a jam or a negative environment is by being very transparent. Call it a red light. Don't call it yellow or green but call it red when it's red and have everyone row against that new goal. There is a lot more upside to being open and honest and sharing everything than the downside associated with hiding and masking it. The upside is that you build a level of trust

and respect and support. To think that everything's perfect and up and to the right all the time for everybody is just not true. There's way too much happy talk in business, but then on Day 1 of the next quarter, there are layoffs and cuts, which creates a whipsaw effect where you blow up trust and respect and loyalty very quickly.

Read the Weather *and* Set the Weather

As we discussed in chapter 5, successful leaders develop a system for listening to know what people are thinking and saying at all levels of the organization. It is the skill of reading a room at an organization-wide level and being able to pick up on the nonverbal cues of body language to understand the subtle emotions at play. CEOs need to be able to sense the mood—to, in effect, "read the weather"—in meetings or as they walk the hallways or visit stores and factory floors. Yet leaders must also recognize that they play an outsized role in setting the weather, because they set the tone through their body language and energy.

For example, Lisa Falzone, the CEO of Athena Security, learned that she had to pay attention to employee morale, but couldn't let it guide her. "You always have to be focused on the vision and what you're trying to accomplish, because if you focus too much on what's going on around you in the moment, sometimes it can tear you off your course," she said. "You always want to have composure in front of your employees. They can tell if you're stressed, and then they feed off that. So if I'm ever stressed, either I try to not show it to my employees, or I go work in my office for a little while. I didn't realize this so much when I started, but everything stems from you."

> "You always want to have composure
> in front of your employees. They
> can tell if you're stressed, and
> then they feed off that."
>
> —Lisa Falzone, cofounder and CEO, Athena Security

Create Freedom *and* Structure

The nature of a leader's work is going to affect the balance of this paradox. In some areas, such as running nuclear power plants and performing surgery, the margin for error is incredibly low, and the culture is necessarily less about freedom and more about structure, more about safety and compliance than creativity and improvisation. In others, like advertising or television, there is much greater need for new ideas, which require a certain amount of chaos to emerge. Big companies may have a mix of both, with more of a process-driven manufacturing arm and a marketing department that demands fresh thinking. For leaders, that means allowing for a certain amount of work that may appear unproductive, with side trips down blind alleys and seemingly unproductive brainstorming. The challenge is knowing when to let the conversation unfold and knowing when to step in to redirect the discussion. Marjorie Kaplan, the former president of global content for Discovery, Inc., said:

> Organizations have a tendency to be self-censoring, always moving forward and making decisions at the exclusion of a kind of tolerance for confusion that I think you need for creativity. You don't want a confused organization all the time. But you can't have an orderly organization all the time, either. Real creativity comes from the ability to tolerate the confusion and to be able, in the right moment, to land the decision and then move forward with that decision in a structured way. My ability to tolerate confusion has grown. Creativity is frightening and messy. You're not going to get a big, game-changing idea from trying to do what you're doing now, but just a little bit better. You must find a way to try ideas that don't seem like they make any sense, to let certain people just go spiraling off for a while, because that's their process. And then decide when it's time to reel them in.

. . .

Now for the final paradox: the very best leaders are selfless—it is not about you, but rather what you can do for the people you lead and for your organization. Yet if you aspire to be that selfless leader, then you must learn to take care of yourself first; otherwise, your physical and emotional energy will be compromised, limiting your ability to help others. So winning the inner game means answering the following questions, among others: How do you manage your ego, which the trappings of leadership have a way of inflating, so that you don't become overly confident and start communicating in ways that are off-putting to people? How do you handle all of the stresses from the endless demands, the weight of expectations, and the consequences of your decisions? How do you remain calm on the outside when you may be in turmoil on the inside? Where do you get the stamina to be your very best, in every encounter, through days of back-to-back meetings with different groups, all of which have outsized expectations of you? How do you make time for yourself so you can reflect beyond the demands and pressures of today to peer over the horizon? How do you nourish yourself in some intellectual or cultural way so that you can feel inspired, to better inspire others? How do you find someone who has no other agenda than to help you and can be a trusted sounding board for your ideas and is willing to simply listen to you vent? How do you take care of your health?

While these pressures are particularly magnified for CEOs, every person in a leadership role experiences them to some degree. Here are some approaches that leaders have adopted for dealing with them.

Acknowledge the Pressures

One trap that leaders can fall into is denial about the stresses of the job. They say to themselves, "I deal with pressure all the time. I love pressure. I eat pressure for lunch." Or their response is one of surrender—"It's part of the job; there's nothing I can do about it"—as if they are simply trying to keep from capsizing during a treacherous white-water rafting trip. Or they defer the work they need to do to restore themselves. "I'll take care of all that stuff later," they tell themselves. "This won't last very long. I'll go on that vacation for a week, and things will be fine."

"The amount of responsibility you carry around on your back is unbelievable."
—William D. Green, former Chairman and CEO, Accenture

These approaches don't work, because the nature of stress is that it's cumulative. Pressures are not just experienced in the moment and then go away; they build on each other, even when things are going well. Now add in the inevitable large and small fires that have to be put out at work. Ideally, those moments of maximum stress would be balanced by relative calm on the home front, yet that never seems to happen; instead, work-life balance becomes perfectly imbalanced, with simultaneous strains at work and at home. Over time, all these pressures start draining your emotional and physical energy reserves and wearing down your resilience. You may have as your highest objective to bring your best self to work every day, yet all the stresses you face will be in opposition to that goal, like a car whose gas tank is low, two cylinders are not firing, and the brakes are seized. Progress will be slow if not impossible.

"The amount of responsibility you carry around on your back is unbelievable," said William D. Green, the former CEO of Accenture. "It's not like you're a martyr—it just comes with the territory. There's something going on around the globe in our place 24/7, and the sense of responsibility you feel for all those people and their families is profound. I like taking the responsibility, but I had no idea about the spiritual part. The spiritual obligation to the lives of so many people is a big deal. I'm a guy who had trouble being responsible for his own life in the early days, and now I've got tens of thousands of people who look up to me. That took a little getting used to."

Keep Your Ego in Check

As people move up the ranks, each promotion carries with it more status markers. A common sign of ego inflation is when leaders, even of small teams, start dropping the phrase "my staff" into conversations, or they substitute "I" for the company instead of "we," because they start thinking that they are fully responsible for the success of the organization. For CEOs, armies of people are deployed to look after and anticipate their every need. Invitations flood in to speak at industry conferences. They become the face of the company, and the lines between the enterprise and their identity blur. For those who tend to take themselves too seriously, all those signals can conspire to inflate their egos to the size of a balloon in a Macy's Thanksgiving Day Parade. It can make them overconfident. It can make them unapproachable. It can make them communicate in an arrogant way so that people don't want to hear them.

Combating those tendencies requires building relationships with a trusted colleague or two who can tell you when you didn't handle a situation as well as you thought. For CEOs, that person may be the chief human resources officer, whose interests span the overall health and effectiveness of the organization. For Kevin, that trusted confidant was Brian McNamee, his head of HR, who would occasionally walk into his office and close the door to deliver some feedback to his boss that usually began with the words, "You let your fastball get away from you again."

For Abbe Raven, the former CEO of A+E Networks, her strategy was always to avoid the "rarefied air" of senior leadership positions. "There are many executives who only travel on private planes, go from office to car to home to a hotel, and you're not really experiencing the world," she said. "I take the train in every day. I look at what people are reading, watching, what devices they're using. I go shopping. I buy the milk in the house. I watch TV. You want to make sure that you're in touch with not only your employees, but also your customers and your viewers, and what they like and don't want. Be out there. Don't let yourself get trapped in your office. You need to be in the world. And the world is not just other executives."

Focus on a Few Achievable Goals

Leaders face so many demands on their time, as well as pressures to set stretch goals that are supposed to inspire everyone to do their best. But such goals can also backfire. If the goal is simply too far out of reach, it will demotivate your team, and you will worry about falling short of expectations. It's better to set goals that are realistic and are in balance between too easy and too ambitious. "One of the things I've really come to appreciate is that you tend to work harder when you're winning," said Andre Durand, the CEO of Ping Identity, a cloud security company. "You have to be careful and thoughtful about the way you set expectations. You don't want them to be slam dunks, but you don't want them to be unattainable, either. They need to be within the realm of attainable. Even though you don't have every step of the way figured out, you're pretty confident that you're matching the resources and the talent and the goals, and that all of those are aligned."

You have to practice the meta work of analyzing how you're spending time to ensure that you're focused on executing the simple plan that you developed with your team. "The best time-management strategy I have," said Wendy Kopp, the founder of Teach For America, "is to reflect an hour a week on the overall strategic plan for myself— what do I need to do to move my priorities forward? And then there are the ten minutes a day that I spend thinking about, 'OK, so based on the priorities for the week, how am I going to prioritize my day tomorrow?' I am obsessive about that system because the world seems to be moving faster and faster, so you have to figure out how to still drive things proactively instead of just becoming completely reactive."

Try to Make Yourself Dispensable

There is a common dynamic that can spring up in organizations where work becomes a kind of Ironman competition, with bragging rights earned by starting earlier, working later, and even giving up part of a vacation to handle a crisis. The impulse is understandable, up to a point, as stamina is an important part of succeeding in senior leadership roles. But it can become a status marker that carries a not-so-subtle message of "I'm so central to the success of this organization that I can't delegate this crucial work to others. If not for me, we would be in trouble."

For new leaders, whose job is now to succeed through others, shifting this mindset can be difficult. But they need to work on making themselves obsolete rather than being considered as essential as air and water to the enterprise. "My view, in the early part of my career, was that appearances mattered, that looking like you're working hard mattered," said Steve Case, the CEO of the investment firm Revolution who is best known as a cofounder of AOL. "But the art is really about trying to set the priorities and assemble a team so you wake up in the morning and actually have nothing to do. It's impossible to achieve, but it's a good goal to have the right priorities and the right team in place so they can execute against those priorities. The objective should not be looking busy, but actually creating a process that allows great things to happen in a way that you can be less involved."

Recharge Yourself

We all know what it feels like when we are at our very best. But the pressures of life and work can make it hard for that person to show up as consistently as we would like. To do so, you must build time into your schedule to stay physically fit, so that it becomes part of your routine. Exercise is just one of the buffers you need to keep the job from becoming all-consuming. You need to make time for the activities that give a sense of self-renewal and inspiration, whether it's from nature, art, movies, or a spiritual practice. It is about being constructively selfish, to know what you want and what you need to restore your emotional resilience to take on the demands of work. It means making time for, and being present with, your family, and staying connected to old friends so that you can remind yourself that the job is part of your life, not your whole life. There will always be something urgent at work that conspires to push these priorities to the sidelines, but you have to provide the counterweight of making them equal priorities.

> **"That's the beauty of the mantle of leadership. You earn it, and every day the clock starts again."**
> **—Michelle Peluso, Chief Marketing Officer, IBM**

With your batteries recharged, you'll be more able to help others, and you can see your challenges through fresh eyes to spot new possibilities and regain clarity about what matters most and why. And you will have the emotional space and time to reflect on what you need to do to become more self-aware and how you can grow and develop as a leader. "From a personal leadership perspective, I think the clock gets reset every morning," said Michelle Peluso, a veteran CEO who is now the senior vice president of digital sales at IBM and its chief marketing officer. "Every night when I go to bed, I think about the things I could have done better—I could have been more empathetic, for example, or I could have been clearer up front about that project, or I should have listened better. That's the beauty of the mantle of leadership. You earn it, and every day the clock starts again. You always have the opportunity to show up better for your teams."

. . .

Given the toll that leadership roles can take on your life, particularly the most senior jobs, is it all worth it? Yes, these positions carry financial rewards, but are they worth the pressures? That is why mastering the inner game of leadership—embracing all the paradoxes, including being constructively selfish in order to be selfless—is so crucial. If you succeed, then you will be able to enjoy the lasting rewards of leadership, including doing important work that requires your very best self, and learning what you're capable of (and it's often more than you thought possible). You will be exposed to a broader range of experiences, giving you the opportunity to constantly learn. You're making some contribution to society, and you have the ability to bring out the best in others. "As the years have gone on, I've really honed my ability to listen and understand everybody's story, and to help them build a story around their capabilities—a story that's open-ended, that plays to their strengths," said Jim Rogers, the former CEO of Duke Energy who passed away in 2018. "One of the biggest things I find in organizations is that people tend to limit their perceptions of themselves and their capabilities. And one of my challenges is to open them up to the possibilities. I have this belief that anybody can almost do anything in the right context."

"I have this belief that anybody can almost do anything in the right context."
—Jim Rogers, former CEO, Duke Energy

You don't need to be a CEO to have that impact on others. Yes, we named this book *The CEO Test* for the reasons we set out in the introduction; by understanding how chief executives navigate the most critical challenges they face, we believe everybody can be a more effective leader, regardless of their title. If you are reading this book, we know that you aspire to a better leader and to achieve more, and possibly even become a CEO someday. That might happen if everything breaks your way, but many factors are beyond your control, like luck, timing, and personal chemistry, that may keep you from achieving the title you want. What is within your control, however, is how you will lead others. Ultimately, that is defined by your choices, not the choices of others, and how you would answer the following questions in those quiet moments when it's just you and the person in the mirror:

- What values are bedrock for you and will never be compromised, regardless of the challenges you face?

189

- Will you see the people who report to you as assets to help you achieve your goals, or will you see your role as unlocking their skills and talents that they may not see in themselves?

- Are you able to embrace all the demands and paradoxes of leadership and recognize that you must be intensely self-aware and see growth as a lifelong journey?

- Are you willing to take full accountability for results, always strive for improvement, and not instinctively blame others when you miss the mark?

- Do you understand that trust is binary and that people either trust you or don't, based on how you act at every moment?

- Do you have the guts and wisdom to make tough and unpopular calls?

- If employees could choose their managers and leaders, would they choose you? And if so, why?

- Do you understand that, despite all the attention leaders get the higher up they go, that ultimately it's not about you?

This is the final CEO test, the one that will determine whether you succeed, on the terms that only you can set for yourself, in becoming the leader you want to be.

Notes

Chapter 1

1. "Our History," McDonald's, accessed September 25, 2020, https://www.mc donalds.com/us/en-us/about-us/our-history.html.

2. "Our Path Forward," New York Times, https://nytco-assets.nytimes.com/m/ Our-Path-Forward.pdf.

Chapter 2

1. Josh Condon, "Watch Uber CEO Travis Kalanick Be a Massive Dick to His Uber Driver," The Drive, February 28, 2017, https://news.yahoo.com/watch-uber-ceo-travis -kalanick-001456675.html.

Chapter 6

1. Dennis Schaal, "Marriott CEO Sorenson Details Crisis Contingency Plans in Emotional Address," Yahoo, March 19, 2020, https://finance.yahoo.com/news/ marriott-ceo-sorenson-details-crisis-161524903.html.

2. Richard Wray, "Deepwater Horizon Oil Spill: BP Gaffes in Full," The Guardian, July 27, 2010, https://www.theguardian.com/business/2010/jul/27/ deepwater-horizon-oil-spill-bp-gaffes.

3. Andrew Pollack, "Amgen Seeks to Reverse Its Bad News," The New York Times, April 17, 2007, https://www.nytimes.com/2007/04/17/business/17place.html.

Chapter 7

1. Satya Nadella, *Hit Refresh: The Quest to Rediscover Microsoft's Soul and Imagine a Better Future for Everyone* (New York: Harper Business, 2017).

Acknowledgments

We hatched the idea for this project over a long breakfast in New York City in 2018, and we are deeply appreciative of everyone who helped us during the long process of turning those early notions into a book.

Our agent, Christy Fletcher, provided crucial guidance early on to help refine our thinking and sharpen the proposal. We are grateful to the entire team at Harvard Business Review Press for their early interest, support, and professionalism at every stage of the process. Adi Ignatius, Melinda Merino, and Scott Berinato are a powerhouse team, and Scott's deft editing touch made the manuscript stronger. And readers of our first draft—Ron Bancroft, Jeanetta Bryant, Peter Chernin, Heather and Dirk DeRoos, Peter and Katie Dolan, Harry Feuerstein, Jim McNerney, David Reimer, and Carol Sharer—provided incisive feedback that helped solidify our approach on key chapters.

Many others have been important influences for us over the years and have helped shape our thinking about what it means to be an effective leader.

From Adam: I'd like to thank everyone at Merryck & Co., and David Reimer and Harry Feuerstein in particular, for sharing their wisdom about the nuances of leadership, corporate cultures and transformations, and what it takes to build effective teams. The former CEOs and global business leaders who are now mentors for Merryck have been generous in sharing their insights from their first-hand leadership experiences and from their mentoring work with senior executives.

Thank you as well to Rick Smith, the chairman of Merryck, who introduced me to David Reimer back in 2012, the first of many conversations with David that led to me joining Merryck in 2017 for a fulfilling new chapter of my career. From all my years of playing sports when I was younger, I developed a deep appreciation of what a team can accomplish when everyone is pulling together, and it is thrilling to play a role in helping build Merryck into a formidable global presence.

Dozens of CEOs I interviewed for my *Corner Office* feature at the *New York Times*, and in my ongoing interview series on LinkedIn, are quoted in these pages, but every single leader I've interviewed—more than six hundred and counting—has contributed powerful insights, compelling stories, and practical tips that inform this book. *Corner Office* was a side project for me at the *Times*, and in my role as an editor, I was lucky to work with, and learn from, some exceptional leaders, particularly Rick Berke, who had a remarkable knack for bringing out the very best in everybody who worked for him.

From Kevin: I'd like to thank Ken Strahm, my first submarine captain, who showed me what a good leader looks like, encouraged me early on, and placed unusual confidence in a young officer. At General Electric, Mike Carpenter gave me, when I was a second-year McKinsey & Company associate, a chance to join a small group on the chairman's staff in the early days of Jack Welch's tenure and watch and learn from the greatest CEO of his era at close range. Mike was the best boss I ever had and taught me how to analyze and describe complex business situations clearly and simply.

The person who most stands out across the range of my experience is Ron Bancroft. He hired me out of the blue at McKinsey almost forty years ago, has been my friend and close adviser over all the ensuing years, and has never hesitated to hold a mirror up to make sure I embraced reality.

Gordon Binder, Amgen's second CEO, took a chance on hiring me in 1992 when the facts of my résumé argued against it, and was my boss and partner for eight years. Jan Rivkin and Nitin Nohria of the Harvard Business School welcomed me onto the faculty as a total rookie and gave me time and encouragement to learn to teach. It was one of the steepest learning curves I've ever faced, and the view was more than worth the climb.

I'd like to thank my colleagues on the Amgen senior staff. We were partners for over a decade, and it was the privilege of my professional life to work together. Because of the leadership of my successor, Bob Bradway, and the current Amgen team, what we built in those early days endures, prospers, and remains true to Amgen's mission to serve patients and be science-based.

. . .

Finally, and this may fall outside the norm of traditional acknowledgments, we'd like to take a few words to give a shout-out to the power of collaboration and teamwork. When we first started talking about this project, we knew each other from several conversations over the years (Adam first met Kevin when he interviewed him for *Corner Office* in 2009), but there were inherent risks in joining forces to write a book.

Would our thinking be aligned about what it means to be an effective leader? Would we be able to work through differences of opinion? Would we see eye to eye on the best approach for structuring and writing the book? The answers turned out to be yes, across the board, and this has been more of a productive partnership than either of us could have hoped.

We learned a lot from each other—any disagreements we had were settled purely on the merits of the ideas, as we kept our egos checked securely at the door—and we ultimately feel that the breadth of Adam's interviews and the depth of Kevin's leadership experience achieved the magic of the sum being greater than the parts. Working on this book together was a profoundly rewarding experience for us, and we sincerely hope that you found it equally rewarding to read.

About the Authors

ADAM BRYANT is managing director of Merryck & Co., a senior leadership development and executive mentoring firm. A veteran journalist, Adam spent eighteen years at the *New York Times* as a reporter and editor, and has conducted in-depth interviews with more than six hundred CEOs and other leaders, starting with the weekly *Corner Office* interview series that he created for the *Times* in 2009. He is the author of two previous books on leadership, including the *New York Times* bestseller *Corner Office: Indispensable and Unexpected Lessons from CEOs on How to Lead and Succeed* and *Quick and Nimble: Lessons from Leading CEOs on How to Create a Culture of Innovation.* He is the senior adviser to the Reuben Mark Initiative for Organizational Character and Leadership at Columbia University.

KEVIN SHARER is the former president, CEO, and chairman of Amgen, the world's largest biotechnology company, and led the company's expansion over two decades from $1 billion to nearly $16 billion in annual revenue. After stepping down from Amgen in 2012, he taught strategy and management at Harvard Business School for seven years and cocreated with his then faculty colleague and current CEO of G.E., Larry Culp, and Nitin Nohria, the Harvard Business

School dean, a popular course on the life and role of the CEO and how to lead senior executive teams. He has served on the boards of Chevron, Unocal, Northrop Grumman, and 3M. In his roles as an executive, director, and mentor, he has been involved with more than twenty successful CEO transitions, and he continues to advise CEOs of global corporations. Kevin is a Naval Academy graduate and served on two attack nuclear submarines.

Index

Index

Index

Index

Index